"The 1% Banker doesn't seek success, they build a legacy that makes success inevitable."

THE 1% BANKER CLUB

The 40 Micro-Decisions That Separate the Best from the Rest in Banking

RISHABH CHUGH

notionpress.com

INDIA · SINGAPORE · MALAYSIA

ISBN
Paperback 979-8-90231-791-3
Hardcase 979-8-90362-254-2

Disclaimer

The views, opinions, and interpretations expressed in this book belong solely to the author and are based on personal experience and observation. They do not represent the views, policies, or positions of the author's current or past employers, clients, or any affiliated institutions.

All examples, scenarios, and illustrations used throughout this work are for general informational and illustrative purposes only. Any names of individuals, customers, or organizations used are entirely fictitious. Any resemblance to actual persons (living or dead), specific businesses, entities, or real-world events is purely coincidental and is not intended to represent any specific individual or organization.

Dedication

With gratitude to God for His blessings and grace.

In loving memory of my father, Raj, whose quiet strength and values remain my steady compass.

To my mother, Asha, for your boundless love and for always seeing the best in me.

To my wife, Laveena, whose support and partnership make every journey meaningful.

And to my son, Reyansh, my constant reminder of what truly matters.

Acknowledgements

This book has been shaped by the people who have enriched my life and the institutions that have defined my career.

My deepest appreciation goes to my extended family for their continuous encouragement, support and the joy they bring to my life—my brother, Rohit; my sister-in-law, Archana; and my nephews, Rayan & Rommel. I am also profoundly grateful to my wife's family, whose warmth and kindness have always been a source of great comfort and strength.

Professionally, I am deeply grateful to the colleagues, mentors, leaders, and teams I have worked with across my career in banking. They entrusted me with responsibility, challenged my thinking, and allowed me to grow through both success and failure. Their confidence, rigour, and expectations sharpened not only my professional judgement but also my sense of accountability.

I also owe a collective debt to the broader community of Indian banking professionals—those who navigate complexity, pressure, and constant change while striving to build institutions and careers of lasting value. Their realities form the living context from which this work draws its meaning.

Finally, my thanks to every reader who engages with these distinctions thoughtfully. If this book prompts even a brief pause before an important decision, it will have fulfilled its purpose.

Table of Contents: The 1% Banker Club

Author's Note: Why I Wrote This Book

This book did not begin as an ambition to write. It began as a pattern I could no longer ignore. This book is written from observation, not instruction.

Over the years, I observed that the most respected and enduring professionals were not always the smartest, the loudest, or the most technically gifted. It wasn't always the person with the highest IQ or the most prestigious degree who ascended to the top 1% of the industry. What separated them was something quieter: the quality of decisions they made when no one was watching—how they spoke, how they chose restraint over reaction, principle over policy, and long-term trust over short-term wins. It is shaped by small, repeated choices—how they think, speak, act, and lead when pressure is highest.

The 1% Banker Club is an attempt to capture those moments. It is not a manual on products, markets, or tactics. It is a study of judgment. Each chapter reflects a distinction I have seen repeatedly shape careers—not in dramatic turning points, but in daily micro-decisions that compound over time.

This book is written for professionals who sense that competence alone is no longer enough, and who want to understand what truly sustains credibility, influence, and legacy in a demanding industry.

Preface: The Banker's Crossroads

When a professional joins the banking industry—a massive global employer for ambitious graduates and post-graduates alike—the early definition of Success is immediate and clear: targets achieved, rapid promotions, and high compensation. This pursuit helps many advance rapidly, delivering immediate results that validate years of dedicated effort.

But what most fail to realize is that this immediate success is often a short-term plateau.

The career path is shaped like a pyramid: wide and welcoming at the base, but narrowing sharply as you approach the peak. Today, the middle layer of that pyramid is growing dangerously congested because technical competence is no longer a differentiator; it is the bare minimum.

The journey from the bottom to the mid-layer can be learned from any standard syllabus, but the ascent from that crowded middle to the Peak—the 1%—is fundamentally different. This final ascent cannot be taught through standard professional courses; it must be developed, deeply nurtured, and consistently translated into a strategic edge.

The majority (the 99%) hit this ceiling because they continue to use yesterday's tools for today's complexities. They run so fast that they forget to reflect, losing the very thing that makes them valuable: their unique professional style–the sum of years of experience meeting customers and navigating complex human dynamics. The few who reach the peak—*the 1% Banker Club—master Strategic Distinction.* They make daily choices not between right and wrong, but between the *merely adequate* approach and the *exponentially better* one. They realize that their true leverage lies in mastering the differences in human strategy.

This book is the direct result of analysing a decade of these strategic contrasts. It is not about finance fundamentals; it is about the *Mastery of Mindset.* As many of you, I am also still learning, but this book is designed to make you *pause and reflect on your style as a banker.* You will encounter every distinction within these pages - when dealing with clients, colleagues, and the ever-changing external dynamic. These are the tools that allow the 1% to utilize their experience, reinforce their unique style, and build an enduring legacy.

I invite you to embrace these distinctions, read them as real-life scenarios, choose the style that resonates with you, and enjoy the journey toward the ultimate professional mastery.

Thanks and Regards

Rishabh Chugh

28th Nov 2025, Bangalore.

Introduction: The Currency of Distinction

The Map and the Compass

The global financial industry is an ocean of competence, navigated daily by millions of professionals who possess the technical knowledge required for the job. They know the models, they can read the markets, and they understand compliance. They have mastered the map. Yet, why do so few—the *1%*—truly steer the direction of the industry, influencing culture, commanding trust, and creating enduring value?

The answer is this: the 99% are proficient map-readers; the *1% Banker Club* has mastered the compass.

The map represents transactional knowledge: the technical skills that get you hired. The compass represents *strategic distinction*: the internal, non-quantifiable framework of judgment, ethics, and leadership that guides your decisions when the map runs out. This gap, between possessing technical competence and wielding strategic influence, is the single greatest barrier to elite performance today.

Moving beyond the Illusion of Complexity

The banking world often rewards complexity, cloaking simple truths in jargon and intricate structures. This creates the illusion that the path to the top is paved with ever more complex knowledge. This is untrue. The true mastery of the *1% Banker Club* lies in the power of *Simplicity*. They do not seek complex solutions; they make simple, powerful choices.

The journey you are about to begin is centred on 40 of these powerful choices. I call them-*The 40 Micro-Decisions That Separate the Best from the Rest in Banking*. Each distinction is a fault line in professional thinking—a moment where one path leads to transactional success and the other leads to transformational *Legacy* . Mastering these 40 points of contrast is the key to unlocking exponential professional growth.

The journey to the *1% Banker Club* is a deliberate choice, not an accident of fate. You do not need to be a CEO to start. You need only the willingness to reflect on the 40 Micro-Decisions you make every single day. Your compass is waiting.

Welcome to **The 1% Banker Club**.

How This Book Is Structured: The Classification

The 4-Part Strategic Framework: The Architecture of Ascent

The structure of this book is designed to mirror the actual journey toward elite banking influence. It guides you through a progressive expansion of your authority—starting from your internal beliefs and ending with your institutional impact.

Part I: The Mindset – Internal Architectures

- *Chapters 1–9*
- *The Focus:* This section is your foundation, focusing on self-mastery. Before you can influence a client or lead a team, you must audit your internal operating system. It addresses the psychological traps—like mistaking activity for progress—that keep the 99% anchored to the mid-tier.
- *The Stitch:* By mastering your internal thought processes, you build the unshakeable certainty required to engage externally in Part II.

Part II: The Dialogue – Communication as Currency

- *Chapters 10–19*
- *The Focus:* Dialogue in banking is not just about exchanging information; it is the primary mechanism for building trust. This part moves you from a "transactional voice" to a "strategic partner" by sharpening your ability to listen, inquire, and assert with precision.

- *The Stitch:* Refined communication converts your analytical brilliance into the long-term client loyalty needed for the high-level strategies in Part III.

Part III: The Action – Salesmanship & Strategic Relationship Mastery

- *Chapters 20–28*
- *The Focus:* This is where internal mindset and external dialogue are translated into commercial outcomes. This section addresses the defining shift of the 1%: moving from "product pusher" to "trusted advisor". It focuses on the psychological nuances of value, luxury client segmentation, and ethical persuasion.
- *The Stitch:* Earning the right to be a client's primary advisor provides the professional runway required to build the enduring character explored in Part IV

Part IV: The Legacy – Ownership, Ethics & Growth

- *Chapters 29–40*
- *The Focus:* This is the final ascent. It moves beyond deals and commissions to focus on character, reputation, and institutional leadership. It explores the non-negotiables: choosing principle over policy and building a team that thrives long after you have stepped away.
- *The Final Destination:* This section defines the difference between a successful career and an enduring legacy—the mark of the 1%.

How to Use This Book: The Anatomy of Each Chapter

To ensure this book serves as a high-performance reference manual rather than a linear narrative, every chapter is built upon a proprietary *3-Section Architecture.* This structure is designed to move you from abstract inspiration to concrete, institutionalized behaviour.

Section 1 : The Foundation (The Anchor & The Hook)

Every chapter begins with The Anchor, a foundational quote that roots the micro-decision in a universal truth. This is followed by a brief *Introduction* that sets the stakes. We then immediately immerse you in a *Use Case Example*—a high-stakes, real-world banking scenario. This ensures the distinction is not just understood, but felt.

Section 2: The Core (Strategic Distinction)

This is the intellectual engine of the chapter. Here, we strip away the jargon to reveal the *Strategic Distinction* between the "merely adequate" approach of the 99% and the "exponentially better" path of the 1%. This section provides the definitions and the rationale required to pivot your professional posture.

Section 3: The Implementation (Key Takeaways & Toolkit)

Knowledge without execution is overhead. Hence, this section translates the strategic distinction into *Key Takeaways*—the essential insights you must internalize. We then provide the *Banker's Toolkit,* consisting of checklists and actionable frameworks designed for immediate application in your next client meeting or internal briefing.

The Final Impression: The Mental Tattoo

Each chapter concludes with a *Mental Tattoo*. This is a single, potent one-liner designed to lodge the strategic lesson permanently in your mind, serving as a mental shortcut when you are under pressure and need to make a split-second decision.

This structure ensures you master the distinction at four distinct cognitive levels: *Inspiration, Observation, Comprehension, and Application.*

PART I:
The Mindset - Internal Architectures

The Architecture of Success

Before a builder can lay a single brick or pour the first slab of concrete, they must first understand the *foundation.* They must ensure the bedrock is stable, the blueprints are sound, and the structural integrity is absolute. For the banker, that foundation is *Mindset.*

This section addresses the critical truth that professional failure rarely starts with the client; it begins internally, with a conceptual flaw in how we think, organize, and present ourselves. If your mindset is shaky—if you confuse productive *Thinking* with paralyzing *Worrying*, or mistake *Knowledge* for *Wisdom*—every external effort will be built upon an unstable base.

The nine distinctions in this Part are designed to be a *diagnostic tool for your internal operating system.* We begin by addressing the traps of the mind (the difference between productive thought and mental paralysis), progress through the efficient organization of time and focus, and culminate in mastering the final external projection of your professional persona (the line between *Confidence and Arrogance).*

Your Progression Through Part I

We follow a natural, ascending flow designed for self-mastery:

1. **Eliminating the Noise (Thinking & Worrying):** We first dissect the most common internal sabotage mechanisms that prevent productive work.
2. **Building Intellectual Capital (Knowledge & EQ):** We then ensure your mental toolkit is correctly balanced, combining factual intelligence (IQ) with relationship

aptitude (EQ) and transforming data (Knowledge) into strategic action (Wisdom).

3. **Applying Internal Structure (Focus & Prioritization):** We teach you how to organize your time and effort effectively, moving from the trap of simply *being busy* to achieving measurable *Progress.*

4. **Projecting the Final Image (Confidence & Perception):** Finally, we equip you to project your mastery externally, ensuring your professional image (Perception) aligns with your performance (Reality) without succumbing to Arrogance.

Mastering Part I ensures that everything you say (Part II) and everything you execute (Part III) is built on unshakable internal certainty.

No.	Core Distinction	The Strategic Progression
1.	Thinking vs. Worrying	Mastering the difference between productive thought and mental paralysis.
2.	Knowledge vs. Wisdom	Transforming acquired data into strategic, applicable insight.
3.	EQ vs. IQ	Balancing technical aptitude with the interpersonal skills required for execution.
4.	Identity(Self-Description) vs. Role (Job -Description)	Defining your personal brand (identity) separate from your job title (role).
5.	Confidence vs. Arrogance	Projecting necessary certainty without sacrificing respect for the client.

No.	Core Distinction	The Strategic Progression
6.	Activity vs. Progress	Ensuring effort leads to results, not just the appearance of busyness.
7.	Focus vs. Efficiency	Prioritizing deep, valuable work over quick task completion.
8.	Time Management vs. Prioritization	Deciding what to do (strategy) before deciding when to do it (logistics).
9.	Risk vs. Threat	Strategically viewing uncertainty and mitigating imminent danger.

CHAPTER 1

Thinking vs. Worrying - The Difference Between Action and Paralysis

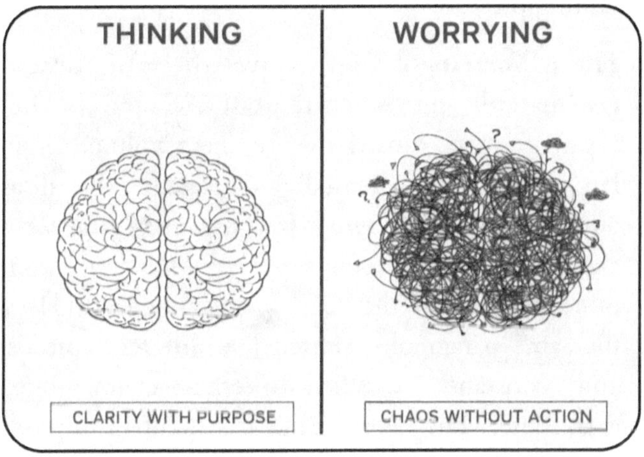

THE ANCHOR

"Thinking moves you toward clarity. Worrying traps you inside uncertainty." — Author

The banker's career is defined by relentless overload: tight deadlines, escalating sales targets month after month, urgent customer escalations, and the pressure of institutional hierarchy. This constant, high-stakes environment often causes a critical internal failure: the substitution of structured thinking with corrosive worrying. Thinking is a structured, problem-solving activity that leads to an action plan. Worrying is a circular, paralyzed mental state that guarantees inaction. This distinction is foundational: you cannot master strategy or dialogue until you master the operation of your own mind.

The Use Case Example: The Frozen Credit Analyst in Chennai

Meet Gaurav, a bright Credit Analyst in Chennai, tasked with conducting due diligence on a major acquisition loan for Astra Logistics. The sheer volume of legal and financial documents, combined with an internal push for immediate sanction, created overwhelming pressure.

- **The Worrying Trap (Overwhelm):** Instead of systematically processing the tasks, Gaurav fell into the cycle of worry caused by the sheer volume of inputs. He spent hours mentally rehearsing the disastrous outcomes: *What if I miss a key covenant? I have three other deadlines and two team meetings; I'll never finish.* The mind focuses on the total, paralyzing load. He reread the same paragraphs, started five different spreadsheets, and constantly checked internal chat groups for reassurance. His "work" time was spent in unproductive mental debate, resulting in the paralysis of analysis. The submission deadline was missed by 48 hours.
- **The Thinking Solution:** Gaurav needed to step back, triage, and action. Productive thinking would have required isolating the biggest risk (the missed covenant), dedicating thirty focused minutes to that task alone, and then returning to the rest of the list.

The failure point was the collapse of the internal operating system. Gaurav was intensely *busy* worrying, but made zero *progress* thinking.

The Strategic Distinction

Thinking is future-oriented and action-focused; Worrying is past-oriented and fear-driven.

Aspect	Worrying (The Mental Trap)	Thinking (The action Lens)
Energy Direction	**Circularity:** Repeating the same negative thought loop without conclusion.	**Linearity:** Structured process with defined inputs and a required output as a solution.
Focus	**Fear & Outcome:** Concentrating on the total overwhelming load.	**Process & Action:** Concentrating on the next manageable step.
Language	**"What if..."** (Hypothetical, paralyzing questions).	**"How to..."** (Actionable, problem-solving questions).
Result	Paralysis, Procrastination, and Missed Deadlines.	Clarity, Decision, and Progress.

The Strategic Analogy: The Financial Modeling Loop

Thinking is like running a financial model iteratively: you input data, test a variable, and generate a new, slightly better result. Worrying is like freezing the model, staring at the screen, and imagining every possible failure scenario without touching the keyboard. Productive thinking requires isolating the current problem and focusing all mental energy on correcting the input, not agonizing over the potential output.

Key Takeaways & The Banker's Toolkit

Key Takeaways

- **Worrying is a cost center; Thinking is a profit center:** Dedicate mental energy only to activities that produce actionable results.
- **The Overload Trap:** The feeling of overwhelm is the signal that you need to stop working and start thinking (triaging).

- **Actionable Question:** Always replace *"What if this defaults?"* with *"What is the single action I can take right now to lower the probability of default?"*
- **Mental Self-Correction:** When you catch yourself worrying, immediately name the emotion, initiate the *Triage system (see below),* and move your physical location.

Quick Action Plan: The 'Overwhelm Triage System'

This three-step system is your immediate action plan when the workload causes you to freeze:

1. **Stop and Capture:** Immediately stop working. Write down *every single task* that is currently worrying you onto a clean sheet of paper (the complete overwhelming list of deadlines, emails, and calls).
2. **Prioritize:** Assign a numeric priority (1, 2, 3) based on the client risk or regulatory deadline, not on volume.
3. **Execute (30-Minute Focus):** Choose the single "1" item and commit to working on *only* that task for 30 minutes. Do not look at emails or the rest of the list. By tackling one piece, you break the paralysis and initiate productive thinking.

Mental Tattoo

Worrying burns time,
Thinking compounds it.

CHAPTER 2

Knowledge vs. Wisdom - The Ultimate Investment in Expertise

THE ANCHOR

"Knowledge accumulates facts, Wisdom filters them before action". — Author

---

In banking, knowledge is easily accessible—a database of market rates, product features, and regulatory guidelines. It is the cost of entry. Wisdom, however, is the rare asset. Wisdom is the strategic, contextual understanding of *when*, *where*, and *how* to apply that knowledge safely and effectively. A banker full of knowledge is a walking textbook; a banker full of wisdom is an indispensable, risk-mitigating partner. In today's dynamic world, where new ways of frauds and financial schemes emerge constantly, it is not just knowledge but wisdom that is needed to read the pattern and see the invisible. This insight must complement the new age banker.

The Use Case Example: The AML Red Flag in Mumbai

Meet Sonia, a sharp, newly recruited MBA graduate in Mumbai, fresh out of orientation and equipped with immense knowledge of the bank's account opening protocols and working capital products. She met with the promoter of Global Infra Solutions, a new firm presenting robust financials, a massive order book, and an urgent need for an account and an immediate working capital line.

- **The Knowledge Trap:** Sonia was highly excited. Her knowledge confirmed the business plan was solid, the projected cash flows justified the loan size, and the internal product parameters fit perfectly. She focused entirely on the numbers and the mechanics of the account opening checklist. Her knowledge convinced her: *This is a great client.*

- **The Wisdom Solution:** Sonia's senior relationship manager reviewed the case and immediately spotted the red flags. The business had no clear digital footprint, the promoter's source of funds was vague, and the rushed urgency was out of sync with standard corporate timelines—all common patterns of potential new age fraud. The senior banker's wisdom, born from years of AML and KYC scrutiny, recognized the pattern of a potentially suspicious shell entity. The senior stepped in, paused the process, and initiated enhanced due diligence, ultimately rejecting the prospect and saving the bank from a severe compliance breach.

The failure point was the substitution of data for insight. Sonia demonstrated strong product knowledge, but had not yet developed the wisdom that comes from understanding institutional risk in full context.

The Strategic Distinction

Knowledge is factual and transferable; Wisdom is contextual and risk-mitigating.

Aspect	Knowledge (The Data Trap)	Wisdom (The Strategic Asset)
Acquisition	**Study:** Gained from textbooks, compliance manuals, and training.	**Experience:** Gained from pattern recognition, market cycles, and learning from past failures.

Aspect	Knowledge (The Data Trap)	Wisdom (The Strategic Asset)
Application	**What:** Knowing *what* product structures are available.	**Why/Context:** Knowing *why* a seemingly perfect product should *not* be used due to unseen risk.
Client Status	**Commodity:** Easily sourced from Google or a competitor's analyst.	**Monopoly:** Cannot be replicated; unique to the experienced banker's judgment.
Outcome	**Information:** Overloading the client with facts.	**Insight:** Mitigating risk and protecting the institution.

The Strategic Analogy: The Surgeon and the Textbook

A medical student has the knowledge of every surgical procedure in the textbook. A surgeon has the wisdom to know that, given this specific patient's underlying history (co-morbidities), the operation is too risky. Wisdom subordinates the technical superiority of a solution to the foundational imperative of risk preservation.

Key Takeaways & The Banker's Toolkit

Key Takeaways

- **Knowledge is a prerequisite; Wisdom is a differentiator:** You must possess the knowledge, but lead with the insight of institutional risk.
- **The Risk Blind Spot:** A perfect-looking business plan can be a knowledge trap. Wisdom demands you look *behind* the numbers for KYC, AML, and source-of-wealth flags—especially regarding new digital fraud patterns.

- **Check Your Ego:** Don't use your technical knowledge to impress; use it to simplify. The best use of knowledge is to identify what to say 'No' to, not what to push.
- **Wisdom is Found in the Client's Story:** Always dedicate more effort to diagnosing the client's source of funds and transactional history than to modeling the product structure.

Quick Action Plan: The 'Simplicity Audit'

1. **Draft:** Create your technical pitch/account opening plan based solely on the numbers and product fit.
2. **Risk Redline:** Review the plan and mentally redline every piece of information that does not align with industry best practices (e.g., rushed timelines, vague funding sources).
3. **Translate to Risk:** If a redlined item causes a moment of doubt, translate the Knowledge (product fit) into a Risk Statement for the Compliance team and pause the process.

> **Mental Tattoo**
>
> **Knowledge informs,**
> **Wisdom decides.**

CHAPTER 3

EQ vs. IQ - The Human Moat Against Automation

THE ANCHOR

"IQ gets the answer right, EQ determines wheather it matters" —Author

---

The banking industry is facing an existential threat from AI and automation. Tools are now capable of executing complex financial modelling, risk analysis, and regulatory compliance (all functions of IQ) with greater speed and accuracy than any human. This technological shift is quickly commoditizing the purely analytical banker. However, the one remaining, irreplaceable source of value in coverage, advisory, and sales is Emotional Intelligence (EQ). The AI may possess the ultimate IQ, but it can never possess the human *E-element*—the ability to connect, empathize, and persuade.

The Use Case Example: The AI-Challenged Client in Hyderabad

Meet Amit, a relationship manager handling mid-market corporate clients in Hyderabad. His bank had recently deployed an AI-driven credit monitoring system designed to flag early warning signals and recommend actions automatically. One of Amit's long-standing clients, Prakash Components, a profitable auto-ancillary manufacturer, was flagged by the system. A recent quarter showed a sharp dip in cash flows, delayed receivables, and a breach of an internal liquidity threshold. The AI-generated recommendation was clear and decisive: *Freeze additional limits, tighten covenants, and initiate an exit plan.* On paper, the model was correct. From a credit-risk perspective, the numbers justified caution.

- **The IQ Trap (The Robot's Strength):** The AI did exactly what it was built to do. It processed historical data, identified stress indicators, benchmarked ratios against industry averages, and generated a risk score that warranted defensive action. What it could not see was context. Amit knew that Prakash Components had recently taken a deliberate hit on cash flows to support a key OEM client during a temporary supply-chain disruption. The receivables were delayed, not impaired. The promoter had injected personal funds quietly to support operations. None of this appeared in the model. The AI saw deterioration. It did not see intent. It saw ratios. It did not see character.
- **The EQ Solution (The Human Moat):** Amit did not challenge the model's math. He did not argue that the ratios were wrong. Instead, he picked up the phone. He spoke to the promoter, the CFO, and later to the procurement head at the OEM. He listened. He connected dots the model could not. He understood the human motivations behind the numbers. When Amit went to the credit committee, he didn't present an emotional plea. He translated human context into institutional comfort:

  "Yes, the cash flows are stressed. But this stress is strategic, temporary, and backed by promoter support. Exiting now protects the spreadsheet—but it damages a ten-year relationship and a fundamentally sound business."

> The committee agreed to maintain limits with tighter monitoring instead of triggering an exit. Six months later, cash flows normalized. The relationship deepened. Amit's value was not in superior analytics. It was in judgment, trust, and contextual understanding—human capabilities no model could replicate.

The failure point was not in the data, but in interpretation. The AI optimized for risk avoidance; Amit optimized for risk understanding. His EQ provided the human moat that turned raw intelligence into sound judgment.

The Strategic Distinction

IQ is the foundation of analytical performance; EQ is the engine of indispensable relationship mastery.

Aspect	IQ (The Analytical Engine)	EQ (The Human Moat)
Foundation	**Data, Logic, Calculations,** and **Technical Expertise** (Commodifiable by AI).	**Context, Empathy, Trust,** and **Pattern Recognition** (Non-commodifiable).
Application	**What:** Knowing the correct formula or product structure.	**Why:** Knowing *why* a client will say yes, despite a better offer.
Client Perception	**Competent** and **Smart** (The price of entry).	**Trusted** and **Indispensable** (The premium differentiator).
AI Threat	**High:** Directly replaceable by algorithmic models.	**Low:** Based on human connection and emotional processing, which AI cannot replicate.

The Strategic Analogy: The Automated Teller vs. The Advisor

IQ is the function of the ATM—fast, reliable, and transactional. EQ is the function of the relationship advisor—the ability to assess unstated needs, manage anxiety, and connect dots across the client's life that no algorithm can see. Focus on the *EQ-driven 20%* of your job (persuasion, diagnosis, trust) that AI can never take, and delegate the *IQ-driven 80%* (data analysis, modelling) to the machines.

Key Takeaways & The Banker's Toolkit

Key Takeaways

- **Your IQ is your floor; your EQ is your ceiling.** AI will force the industry to compete only on the ceiling.
- **The AI Stress Test:** If your value proposition to the client can be replicated by a single report, your job is at risk. Your value must be in managing the client's reaction to the report.
- **The E-Element:** True EQ is the ability to prioritize the client's emotional risk (e.g., job security) over the bank's technical optimization.
- **Never Compete with the Robot:** If an AI model offers a better solution on price or speed, do not argue the numbers. Pivot immediately to the human factors that matter: stability, trust, and relationship-specific context.

Quick Action Plan: The 'Contextual Overlay'

1. **Acknowledge the IQ:** Verbally validate the quality of the data or the AI report ("This model is 99% accurate on cost savings...").

2. **Apply the EQ Pivot:** Immediately introduce the human factor: "Now, let's apply the human overlay. What internal political obstacles or cultural challenges does this recommendation create for you, personally?"
3. **Co-Create:** Work *with* the client to adapt the technical solution (IQ) to their personal comfort level (EQ).

Mental Tattoo

IQ opens the door,
EQ decides who stays.

CHAPTER 4

Identity (Self-Description) vs. Role (Job-Description) - The Difference Between Your Story and Your Title

---

THE ANCHOR

"Tell me the facts and I'll learn. Tell me the truth and I'll believe. But tell me a story and it will live in my heart forever."
— Ancient Proverb

In today's interconnected world, professionals risk becoming indistinguishable. We are so absorbed by our *Role*—our title, our designations, our brand for which we work, our job description—that we lose our *Identity*. Yet, clients are not investing capital in a company; they are betting on a person. The Role gets you in the door; the Identity builds the essential trust, compassion, and recall value. The banker who can strategically weave their personal story into the professional narrative creates a unique human connection that no competitor can commoditize.

The Use Case Example: The Dispassionate Investment Banker in Mumbai

Meet Gautam, a meticulous Investment Banker in Mumbai, pitching for a high-value merger and acquisition (M&A) advisory mandate to the Jain Group, a prominent NRI client based in Dubai. Gautam prepared an immaculate presentation detailing his Role: transaction volume, firm rankings, and his CV highlighting his degree and experience. He spoke only about the market, the deal structure, and his team's capabilities.

- **The Role Trap:** Gautam executed his role perfectly, but he made no human connection. When the client founder, Mr. Jain, casually asked about his hometown, Gautam gave a clipped, single-sentence answer and immediately pivoted back to the financing structure. The client walked away feeling that while Gautam was technically sound, he was emotionally hollow—a human automaton interchangeable with any other bank's M&A team.
- **The Identity Solution:** The competitor who won the mandate was equally skilled but took five minutes to talk about his wife's teaching career and his passion for collecting classic Indian cinema posters—both points Mr. Jain found common ground with. The competitor built a foundation of Identity (a fellow human with shared interests) before presenting his Role (the financing strategy). The Jain Group chose the competitor because they trusted the person they felt gravitated toward, ensuring higher recall value.

The failure point was that Gautam saw the meeting as a technical transaction, not a human interaction. He presented his title, but failed to establish his story.

The Strategic Distinction

Your Identity is your unique, un-commodifiable value; your Role is your organizational function.

Aspect	Role (Job Description)	Identity (Self-Description)
Foundation	**Job Description, CV, Title,** and **Bank Mandate** (Commodifiable).	**Story, Values, Interests,** and **Personal Background** (Un-commodifiable).
Function	Defines your **competence** (What you can do).	Defines your **relatability** (Who you are).
Client Status	**Transactional:** The reason they meet you.	**Foundational:** The reason they trust you and remember you.
Communication	Formal, Technical, and Objective.	Informal, Contextual, and Emotional.

The Strategic Analogy: The Financial GPS

The Role is the destination entered into the GPS—it defines the goal (the deal). The Identity is the voice and personality guiding you there—it defines the experience and establishes trust throughout the journey. The client must know that the person guiding them is reliable, authentic, and connected to the real world. Identity is the storytelling element that guarantees trust.

Key Takeaways & The Banker's Toolkit

Key Takeaways

- **Your Role is interchangeable; your Identity is unique:** Invest effort in defining and presenting your authentic self.
- **The Recall Gap:** Clients forget deal terms and titles, but they remember shared stories and common vulnerabilities. Use your Identity to create *mental markers.*

- **Identity is the Foundation of Compassion:** Personal vulnerability fosters compassion, which bridges the gap during inevitable deal setbacks.
- **Strategic Introduction:** Start every relationship by dedicating a mandatory two minutes to establish common ground before launching into the technical pitch.

Quick Action Plan: The 'Identity Weave'

1. **Define Your 3 Non-Banking Pillars:** Identify three genuine interests or background elements (e.g., family history, passion project, unique skill).
2. **The Contextual Bridge:** Never interrupt the flow to drop an Identity point. Wait for a natural *Contextual Bridge* (e.g., "The market uncertainty reminds me of when my family's old business faced a sudden regulatory change...").
3. **The Close:** When the client shows interest in your Identity point, give a brief, honest reply, and then smoothly pivot back to the Role ("That experience taught me the value of stability, which is why I am recommending this stable financing structure...").

> **Mental Tattoo**
>
> **Your Role gets the meeting,**
> **Your Story gets the mandate.**

CHAPTER 5

Confidence vs. Arrogance: The Fine Line Between Certainty and Dismissal

THE ANCHOR

"Arrogance is Confidence that stopped listening" — Author

For the banker, confidence is the essential currency of the deal. Clients are investing capital based on your assurance, your analysis, and your strategic recommendation. However, when confidence loses its humility and curiosity, it instantly mutates into arrogance. Confidence opens doors; arrogance slams them shut. The distinction is subtle but absolute: Confidence is internal certainty communicated with respect; arrogance is external superiority communicated with dismissal.

The Use Case Example: The Wealth Management Pitch in Hyderabad

Meet Fahad, a high-achieving Private Wealth Manager in Hyderabad, pitching comprehensive portfolio management to Mrs. Revathi Krishna, a retired corporate executive with a significant, diverse personal portfolio.

- **The Arrogance Trap:** Fahad began his pitch by immediately pointing out the flaws in Mrs. Krishna's current, self-managed portfolio. He spoke quickly, using highly technical jargon (e.g., "alpha decay," "structured derivative overlay"), and frequently interrupted Mrs. Krishna when she attempted to explain her historical investment rationale. His underlying message was clear: his expertise mattered more than her experience.." He was certain he was right, but his delivery was dismissive, demonstrating a lack of respect for her past successes.

- **The Lost Opportunity:** Mrs. Krishna was intellectually capable and simply wanted a professional partner. Fahad's arrogance cost him the opportunity. She declined the proposal, not because of the portfolio strategy, but because she felt unheard, patronized, and alienated. She needed *confidence (certainty in the strategy)*, but received *arrogance (certainty in his own superiority)*. A truly confident wealth manager would have first validated her successful track record, *then* asked diagnostic questions, and *finally* presented the bank's solution as an evolutionary step, not a corrective indictment.

The Strategic Distinction

Confidence is built on preparation and shared understanding; arrogance is built on assumption and intellectual isolation.

Aspect	Arrogance (The Trap)	Confidence (The Trust Builder)
Foundation	**Assumption:** Believing you have all the answers before listening.	**Preparation:** Knowing the material, yet being open to new information.
Communication	**Monologue:** Interrupting and using unnecessary jargon.	**Dialogue:** Listening intently and using clear, accessible language.

Aspect	Arrogance (The Trap)	Confidence (The Trust Builder)
Client Perception	**Dismissive** and **Patronizing** (They feel belittled).	**Authoritative** and **Reassuring** (They feel safe).
Goal	To prove **superiority**.	To establish **credibility**.

The Strategic Analogy: The Financial Navigator

The difference is how you hold the map. An arrogant banker throws the client's existing map away and announces, "My map is better." A confident banker reviews the client's map first, validates its successful parts, and then calmly says, "We share your destination. Our map is updated with the latest regulatory and market terrain, and here is how we can navigate the risks together." Confidence invites the client onto the journey; arrogance demands the client follow.

Key Takeaways & The Banker's Toolkit

Key Takeaways

- **Confidence is silent; Arrogance is loud:** You don't need to announce your expertise; your preparation and listening skills should demonstrate it.
- **The Rule of Validation:** Start every diagnosis with validation. Acknowledge the client's current success or existing decisions before presenting a correction or change.
- **Jargon is Arrogance in Disguise:** Use simple, direct language. Jargon is a cheap tool to mask uncertainty or establish false superiority.
- **The Best Confident Bankers** are those who are not afraid to say, "I don't know, but I will find out by the end of the day."

Quick Action Plan: The 'Humble Authority' Check

1. **Validate First:** Begin the meeting by asking the client, "What part of your current strategy has been most successful, and why?"
2. **Jargon Filter:** If you use a technical term (e.g., "synthetic hedge"), immediately follow it with: "Does that term make sense, or should I explain it differently?"
3. **Pause and Listen:** After delivering a key recommendation, pause for a full three seconds. Do not fill the silence. This demonstrates you are confident enough to let your recommendation stand on its own merit, inviting dialogue, not rebuttal.

Mental Tattoo

Confidence invites trust,
Arrogance invites resistance.

CHAPTER 6

Activity vs. Progress - The Difference Between Motion and Movement

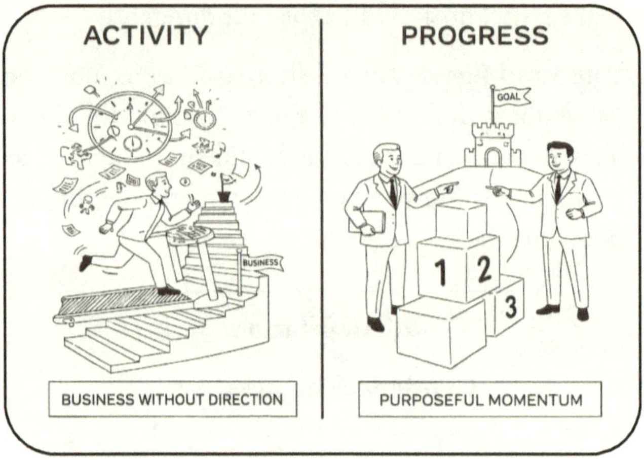

THE ANCHOR

"It's not enough to be busy, so are the ants. The question is: what are we busy about?" — Henry David Thoreau

The banking environment often leads to a critical failure: confusing Activity with Progress. Activity is the measurable motion—emails sent, meetings attended, or time spent meticulously formatting documents. Progress is the measurable advance toward a strategic goal. The most dangerous form of this trap is *non-productive activity*—the art of *"appearing productive without creating progress"* which masquerades as professionalism. The key insight is that while productive, necessary tasks can sometimes take a long time to yield output, this chapter's critique is aimed at the low-value motion that serves only to justify time spent.

The Use Case Example: The Drowning Relationship Manager in Kolkata

Meet Debjit, a Corporate Relationship Manager in Kolkata, whose performance had plateaued despite working 60-hour weeks. He was always active but showed little progress toward his quarterly sales target. His client was Eastern Chemicals, a major manufacturing client needing a Trade Finance facility.

- **The Activity Trap (Non-Productive Motion):** Debjit's workday was filled with motion that allowed him to *"look busy and avoid the hard work."* He spent two hours meticulously formatting an internal credit memo, using custom fonts and detailed charts—a task that should have taken 15 minutes and added no value to the risk decision. He spent an hour in a non-mandatory product training meeting and checked his Bloomberg terminal sixty times (market noise). He *felt* busy and looked responsive to his team, but zero hours were spent on the one productive activity that mattered: client interaction, tailored pitch construction, or high-value cross-selling analysis. This non-productive activity consumed his energy without advancing the Trade Finance deal.
- **The Progress Solution (Trackable Movement):** A focus on Progress would have dictated: Spend 15 minutes formatting the memo, delegate the compliance check, and use the saved 90 minutes to design three bespoke Trade Finance scenarios for Eastern Chemicals based on their shipping routes. Progress is measured by the *distance moved toward the goal (closer to the signature),*

not by the calories burned (emails sent). This shift—from visible activity to measurable progress—did more than revive the Trade Finance deal. It made Debjit visible again as a banker who delivered outcomes, not just effort.

The failure point was that Debjit allowed low-value internal activity to masquerade as professional progress, resulting in a plateaued career.

The Strategic Distinction

Activity is the visible effort; Progress is the visible, trackable result.

Aspect	Activity (The Mask)	Progress (The Outcome Lens)
Focus	**Effort & Input:** Emails, meetings, formatting, or the act of **"looking busy."**	**Result & Output:** Deal signature, risk mitigation, mandate earned, client trust deepened.
Value Type	**Can be Non-Productive:** Often low-value internal administration or compliance dressed up as essential work.	**Always Productive:** Directly moves the needle on strategic, revenue, or risk goals, regardless of the time required.
Measurement	**Time Spent** (Hours worked, meetings attended).	**Distance Moved** (Percentage complete, client decision achieved).
Consequence	**Burnout:** Energy expended without professional advancement.	**Advancement:** Energy converted into measurable career momentum.

The Strategic Analogy: The Financial GPS vs. The Treadmill

Activity is running on a treadmill: you are moving fast, expending energy, and generating heat, but you are still in the same spot. Progress is setting a point on the GPS and advancing toward the destination. The career mistake is confusing the *treadmill time (internal reports) for the GPS movement (client interaction).*

Key Takeaways & The Banker's Toolkit

Key Takeaways

- **Productive Activity is the only kind that counts:** Non-productive activity—especially the act of *"looking busy"*—is a strategic distraction.
- **The Banker's KPI:** Stop measuring your day by the time logged and start measuring it by the *key decisions secured (internal or external).*
- **The Art of Saying No:** The single greatest driver of progress is the ability to politely but firmly decline *non-productive activities* (e.g., non-mandatory meetings).
- **Deep Work vs. Non-Productive Activity:** Distinguish between a complex, necessary task (e.g., modelling a debt structure that takes two days) and low-value, optional administrative work (e.g., over-formatting a low-stakes memo). Only the latter should be ruthlessly eliminated.

Quick Action Plan: The 'Progress Audit'

1. **Map the Goal:** Identify the one crucial result needed this week (e.g., "Finalize Trade Finance terms with Eastern Chemicals").

2. **Define the Next Action:** List the 3-5 necessary actions required (e.g., Call CFO, Draft term sheet, Get credit approval).

3. **Audit the Rest:** For every incoming request (email, meeting, memo), ask: *"Does this move me closer to the Trade Finance signature? Yes or No?"* If the answer is No, it is a low-value activity that must be delegated or deleted.

Mental Tattoo

Activity is motion,
Progress is movement.

CHAPTER 7

Effectiveness vs. Efficiency - The Difference Between Doing the Right Things and Doing Things Right

---

THE ANCHOR

"The main thing is to keep the main thing the main thing."
— Stephen Covey

In the modern banking office, efficiency is revered: clear the inbox, complete the checklist, finish the presentation quickly. But efficiency is a trap if applied to the wrong task. Effectiveness—the discipline of choosing the right work—is the higher-order skill. Efficiency is about speed (how fast you run); Effectiveness is about judgment (which direction you run). A banker must ruthlessly prioritize the deep, complex analysis that drives strategic value and deliberately batch or delegate the high-speed, routine tasks that consume time without advancing the strategic relationship.

The Use Case Example: The Overwhelmed Wealth Manager in Bengaluru

Meet Avantika, a highly organized Wealth Relationship Manager in Bengaluru, serving ultra-HNIs. Her primary client, Mr. Rao, had just inherited a significant offshore asset requiring complex, multi-jurisdictional tax optimization *(the High-Effectiveness Task).* Simultaneously, her manager handed her a list of fifteen routine client trading orders that needed processing before market close *(the High-Efficiency Task).*

- **The Efficiency Trap:** Avantika, driven by her desire for a clean task list, prioritized efficiency. She knew she could execute the fifteen trading orders in a rapid, high-speed burst. This gave her the immediate satisfaction of completion and the visible reassurance of responsiveness. She deferred the Rao tax case—which required her phone to be off and a dedicated three hours of uninterrupted, deep work.
- **The Focus Failure:** She executed the orders flawlessly. However, by the time she returned to the Rao tax case late in the day, her cognitive energy was depleted. The repetitive, high-speed execution had consumed her attention and mental bandwidth.

As a result, she approached a high-judgment problem in a low-energy state. Distracted by new emails, she fragmented her attention into two shallow one-hour blocks instead of one sustained deep-work session. In this fatigued condition, she missed a crucial detail related to a tax treaty application. The error was minor in form but significant in consequence, immediately damaging Mr. Rao's trust in her strategic competence. The failure was not due to a lack of speed, but a lack of effectiveness—misjudging which task deserved her best cognitive energy and when that energy should have been spent.

The failure point was misapplying efficiency to a strategic task. Avantika excelled at low-judgment, high-speed work but failed at the high-judgment, low-speed work that generates premium value.

The Strategic Distinction

Effectiveness determines what to work on; Efficiency determines how fast the work is executed.

Aspect	Efficiency (The Speed Trap)	Effectiveness (The Leverage Lens)
Goal	**Speed and Quantity:** Maximizing output per hour; clearing the task list.	**Judgment and Impact:** Identifying and solving the highest-leverage problem.
Required Mindset	**Multitasking:** Rapid context switching; constant responsiveness.	**Prioritization**: Single-tasking on the most consequential issue.
Value to Client	**Tactical**: Timely execution of routine requests.	**Strategic**: Unique problem-solving and risk mitigation.
Relationship Impact	**Commodity**: Makes you fast, but interchangeable.	**Indispensable**: Makes you trusted and difficult to replace.

The Strategic Analogy: The Financial Calculator vs. The Whiteboard

Efficiency is using a financial calculator—it is fast, immediate, and executes known formulas quickly. Effectiveness is standing at a whiteboard—it is slower, requires sustained concentration, and is used only to solve a novel, complex problem that the calculator cannot handle. Bankers must learn to dedicate protected time to the whiteboard and not allow calculator tasks to dominate the day.

Key Takeaways & The Banker's Toolkit

Key Takeaways

- **Effectiveness precedes efficiency.** Never apply speed to a problem that has not been correctly prioritized.
- **The Energy Blind Spot:** Doing easy work first often drains the very cognitive energy required for complex, high-value decisions.

- **Where Value Is Created:** Time spent on judgment-heavy work (tax structuring, complex modelling, strategic pitch design) is what generates premium client trust and fees.
- **Protected Time Is Non-Negotiable:** You must deliberately shield time for the single most important task of the day.

Quick Action Plan: The 'Effectiveness Block'

1. **Identify the Effectiveness Task:** At the start of the day, identify the single most complex, non-routine, revenue- or risk-critical task (the *Whiteboard Task*).
2. **Quarantine the Time:** Block a minimum 90-minute uninterrupted window in your calendar and turn off email and chat notifications. This is protected judgment time.
3. **Batch Efficiency:** Schedule all routine, high-speed tasks (emails, processing, approvals) into a single Efficiency Block after the Effectiveness Task is complete.

Mental Tattoo

Efficiency handles the volume,
Effectiveness handles the value.

CHAPTER 8

Time Management vs. Prioritization - Value Over Urgency

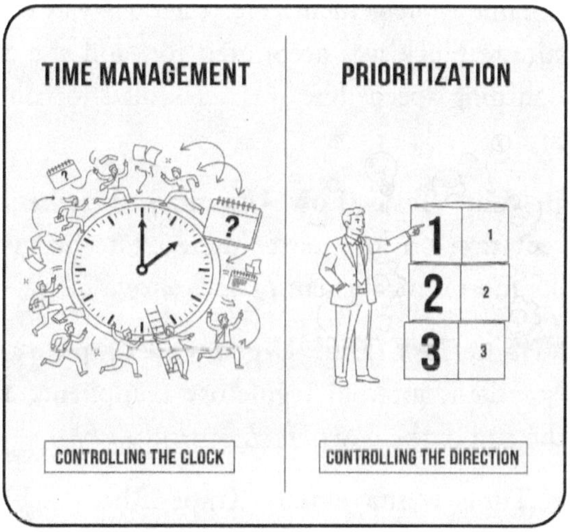

THE ANCHOR

> "The key is not to prioritize what's on your schedule, but to schedule your priorities." — Stephen Covey

In a high-stakes environment, the banker's ultimate constraint is not capital or headcount—it is time. Most professionals attempt to solve this by mastering Time Management (the logistics of scheduling and efficiency). But effective scheduling is useless if you are scheduling the wrong things. Prioritization is the higher-order skill that dictates value; it is the strategic decision to execute the most impactful task, even if it is complex and uncomfortable. Time management is a tool; Prioritization is a strategy.

The Use Case Example: The Flawless but Failed Schedule in Hyderabad

Meet Rhea, a Treasury Sales Manager in Hyderabad, who was a master of Time Management. Her calendar was color-coded, every 30-minute block was accounted for, and she cleared her emails at lightning speed. She was scheduled to complete two major tasks:

1. **High-Value Task (Low Urgency):** Prepare a bespoke presentation on long-term interest rate hedging for the bank's most critical client *(The Strategic Task).*
2. **Low-Value Task (High Urgency):** Complete and submit 15 standard, internal regulatory compliance forms due by the end of the day *(The Logistical Task).*

- **The Time Management Trap:** Rhea's schedule was perfectly executed. She chose to start her day by clearing the highly urgent compliance forms because they were easier to complete, carried an end-of-day deadline, and helped clear her internal task list early. Importantly, the deadline did not require immediate execution—only completion by day's end—but urgency created the illusion that it had to be addressed first. She was an impeccable time manager. However, by front-loading the low-value administrative work, she pushed the high-value interest rate presentation to the evening, when her cognitive energy was depleted and her thinking was rushed.
- **The Prioritization Failure:** Rhea's lack of prioritization meant the strategic interest rate hedge presentation

was delivered with sloppy analysis and errors. The client detected the lack of focused effort and passed the mandate to a competitor. Rhea perfectly managed her time, but she scheduled the tasks based on *perceived urgency (the internal deadline) rather than value (the client relationship and revenue impact).* She failed to recognize that a perfect schedule of the wrong tasks is still a failure.

The failure point was that Rhea's *Time Management* skills failed to compensate for her *Prioritization* flaw.

The Strategic Distinction

Prioritization dictates the value; Time Management dictates the speed of delivery.

Aspect	Time Management (The Logistic Trap)	Prioritization (The Strategic Asset)
Core Question	**How** do I fit everything in? (Scheduling, Organization, Speed).	**What** should I do right now that drives the highest value? (Strategy, Impact).
Driving Force	**Urgency** (Loud emails, hard deadlines, internal pressure).	**Value** (Revenue impact, risk mitigation, strategic client retention).
Output	**Volume:** Completing the entire checklist quickly.	**Impact:** Securing the largest return on invested time.
Banker's Status	**Efficient Operator** (Exchangeable).	**Strategic Decision-Maker** (Indispensable).

The Strategic Analogy: The Plane's Route vs. The Plane's Speed

Time Management is controlling the speed of the plane to ensure it flies as fast as possible. Prioritization is controlling the navigation system to ensure the plane is flying toward the correct city. A perfectly time-managed day spent completing low-value internal work is like flying at maximum speed toward the wrong destination. Always let the Prioritization (the map) determine your Time Management (the speed).

Key Takeaways & The Banker's Toolkit

Key Takeaways

- **Prioritization is the Master Skill:** Time Management is just the execution tool.
- **Value over Urgency:** Never schedule a task based on how loud its deadline is. Schedule based on the revenue or risk impact on the client.
- **The Uncomfortable Task:** The most highly prioritized tasks (e.g., complex analysis, difficult client calls) are often the ones that feel the most uncomfortable or lack a hard deadline. These are the tasks that create value.
- **Don't Fear the Incomplete Checklist:** It is better to leave one low-value administrative task incomplete at the end of the day than to rush a high-value strategic deliverable.

Quick Action Plan: The 'Banker's V-U Matrix (Value – Urgency Matrix)

Inspired by the *Eisenhower prioritization framework,* this Banker's V-U Matrix redefines urgency through the lens of value creation and risk management

To achieve true strategic prioritization, use this matrix, which combines the two decisive factors in banking:

Urgency \ Value	High Value	Low Value
High Urgency	**Quadrant 1: STRATEGY (Act Now)** • Client retention issues • Compliance breaches • Market risk exposure fixes	**Quadrant 3: ADMINISTRATION (Delegate / Minimize)** • Internal non-compliance forms • Routine approvals • Non-critical internal escalations
Low Urgency	**Quadrant 2: VALUE CREATION (Schedule First)** • Strategic pitch decks • Hedging strategy design • Succession or capital-structure analysis	**Quadrant 4: NOISE (Eliminate / Avoid)** • Market email clutter • Optional internal meetings • Low-impact updates

The Banker's Rule: Spend your best cognitive time (early morning) on *Quadrant 1* and *Quadrant 2* tasks only. Use Quadrant 3 only to delegate.

Mental Tattoo

What is important is seldom urgent,
What is urgent is seldom important.

CHAPTER 9

Risk vs. Threat - The Difference Between a Calculated Exposure and an Existential Event

---

THE ANCHOR

"Risk is uncertainty you choose to manage. A threat is uncertainty you failed to prepare for."— Author

---

For a banker, everything is measured against the balance of exposure and reward. However, the professional must distinguish between the two primary sources of uncertainty: *Risk and Threat.* Risk is a quantifiable exposure—it is inherent to the business, can be modeled in a spreadsheet, and can be priced into a product (e.g., a higher interest rate). Threat is an unquantifiable, external event—it is existential, sudden, and often institutional (e.g., a geopolitical crisis or a sudden regulatory ban). The average banker focuses on Risk; the strategic banker manages for the Threat.

The Use Case Example: The Unforeseen Regulatory Freeze in Delhi

Meet Vikas, a seasoned Corporate Relationship Manager in Delhi, responsible for managing a large portfolio of infrastructure clients. His biggest client, Northern Structures, needed a ₹200 Crore term loan.

- **The Risk Management (Quantifiable):** Vikas meticulously managed the Risk. He noted Northern

Structures' high Debt-to-Equity ratio, a slight reliance on a single vendor, and volatility in the steel market. He correctly modeled the exposure, added stringent covenants, and priced the loan 150 basis points higher to compensate for the calculated financial Risk. The bank was protected against the typical business failure.

- **The Threat Event (Unquantifiable):** Three months later, the central government—due to environmental concerns—issued an immediate moratorium (a sudden, unexpected Threat) on all new construction projects in Northern Structures' primary operating region. The company instantly lost its entire revenue stream, making the loan non-performing, regardless of Vikas's excellent financial modelling. Vikas had successfully managed the financial Risk of the client's balance sheet, but he had failed to anticipate the existential Threat of a non-financial, political and regulatory event.

The failure point was misclassifying the danger. Vikas treated an unquantifiable *Threat (regulatory stability) as a manageable Risk (balance sheet health),* proving that perfect modelling cannot save a bank from a systemic shock.

The Strategic Distinction

Risk is quantifiable, can be priced, and is inherent to business; Threat is existential, unquantifiable, and must be avoided.

Aspect	Risk (The Exposure)	Threat (The Event)
Quantification	**Measurable:** Can be modeled, assigned a probability, and charged a premium (e.g., VaR).	**Unquantifiable:** Sudden, unexpected, and systemic; cannot be priced effectively.

Aspect	Risk (The Exposure)	Threat (The Event)
Mitigation Tactic	**Price it and Manage it:** Use covenants, collateral, or higher rates.	**Avoid it and Plan for it:** Use geopolitical/ regulatory intelligence and off-ramps (contingency plans).
Source	**Internal/Business:** Driven by client behavior, competition, or market cycles.	**External/Systemic:** Driven by politics, technology, natural disaster, or regulation.
Goal	To create **profit** by accepting calculated exposure.	To create **survival** by avoiding existential damage.

The Strategic Analogy: The Ship and the Iceberg

Managing Risk is ensuring your ship has sufficient ballast and cargo insurance against high waves and high winds (known exposures). Threat is the unseen iceberg—a sudden, systemic event that can sink the ship instantly. A strategic banker ensures the systems are in place not just to weather the storm (manage the Risk) but also to spot the unexpected iceberg (mitigate the Threat).

Key Takeaways & The Banker's Toolkit

Key Takeaways

- **The Banker's Commodity is Risk:** You are paid to model and accept Risk; you are judged on your ability to avoid Threats.
- **Risk is Internal; Threat is External.** Always look beyond the client's balance sheet to the regulatory, geopolitical, and technological landscape for existential dangers.

- **The Threat Question:** When structuring a deal, always ask: *"What external, non-financial event could instantly make this client or this product worthless?"*
- **The Hedge:** You hedge against Risk with financial products; you hedge against Threat with intelligence and contingency plans.

Quick Action Plan: The 'Threat Scenario Audit'

1. **Identify the Unthinkable:** For your core portfolio, list the single biggest non-financial external event that could instantly zero out the client's value (e.g., Regulatory ban, Cyber breach, Geopolitical sanction).
2. **Define the Off-Ramp:** For each Threat, define the immediate, pre-agreed Off-Ramp (contingency plan). This is not a financial covenant; it's a "what-if" plan.
3. **Stress Test:** Model a scenario where the client defaults, *not* because of their business performance, but because the Threat materialized overnight. This informs your due diligence process.

Mental Tattoo

Risk has a premium,
Threat has consequences.

PART II:
The Dialogue - Communication as a Currency

The Banker's Currency: Trust

If *Part I (The Mindset)* addressed the internal architecture of success, *Part II* moves to the external mechanism of delivery: *The Dialogue.* In banking, dialogue is not merely a tool for conveying information; it is the *currency of trust.* You can have the most brilliant financial strategy (Mindset), but if you cannot articulate it clearly, diagnose the client's unspoken fears, or listen strategically, the strategy remains worthless.

The ten distinctions in this Part teach the mastery of interaction, moving the banker from a transactional voice to an indispensable partner. Every word, every question, and every moment of silence must be intentional.

Your Progression Through Part II

This section is structured to follow the logical flow of a high-stakes professional interaction, starting with reception and ending with correction:

1. **The Foundational Skills (Listening & Inquiry):** We start by dissecting the most basic, yet most often failed, communication skill: how to *Listen* and ask the right *Inquiry* to unlock the client's true needs.
2. **Building Relatability (Empathy & Trust):** We then ensure your message is received correctly by differentiating emotional responses *(Empathy vs. Sympathy)* and separating fact-based belief *(Credibility)* from behavioural connection *(Trust).*
3. **Delivering the Message (Clarity & Non-Verbal):** This section sharpens the delivery, ensuring the client is empowered by *Clarity* and that your message is supported by your *Non-Verbal* presence.

4. **Managing Conflict & Correction (Assertion & Feedback):** We conclude with the mastery of high-stakes dialogue, teaching you how to *Assert* your position firmly and how to use conversation to drive performance improvement *(Feedback vs. Criticism).*

Mastering the distinctions in *Part II* is what converts your analytical brilliance into earned revenue and long-term client loyalty.

No	Core Distinction	The Strategic Progression
10.	Listening vs. Hearing	The foundational skill: moving from passive intake to active, strategic engagement.
11.	Inquiry vs. Assumption	The critical pivot: ensuring you ask the right questions after you listen.
12.	Empathy vs. Sympathy	Using dialogue to diagnose the client's problem, not just acknowledge their pain.
13.	Trust vs. Credibility	Building belief through consistent behavior and factual proof.
14.	Clarity vs. Jargon	Mastering the delivery of complex ideas in simple, empowering language.
15.	Verbal vs. Non-Verbal Communication	Controlling the entire message, including the banker's body language.
16.	Assertion vs. Aggression	Delivering a firm, strategic stance without alienating the counterparty.
17.	Response vs. Reaction	The final strategic choice in dialogue: controlling composure in high-stakes moments.
18.	Feedback vs. Criticism	Using dialogue to drive process and performance improvement (internal/external).
19.	Curiosity vs Interrogation	Uncovering truth through genuine interest, without triggering defensiveness or resistance.

CHAPTER 10

Listening vs. Hearing - The Difference Between Processing Words and Diagnosing Need

THE ANCHOR

"The most important thing in communication is hearing what isn't said." — Peter Drucker

In today's dialogue-saturated world, the professional banker is trained to be a talker—a pitcher of products, a presenter of data. This has led to the critical flaw of confusing Hearing with Listening. Hearing is the passive, physiological act of processing sound. Listening is the active, cognitive process of diagnosing intent, context, and need. The failure to listen happens when the banker is merely *waiting for their turn to speak*, rehearsing their next sentence, and missing the subtle cues that reveal the client's true problem. The greatest opportunity to connect is lost the moment you stop listening to *understand* and start listening only to *reply*.

The Use Case Example: The Pitch-Perfect Failure in Mumbai

Meet Nandini, a bright Relationship Manager in Mumbai, pitching a complex wealth transfer structure to Mr. and Mrs. Desai, a successful entrepreneurial couple planning their succession. Nandini had spent hours memorizing the product details and had a perfectly crafted pitch.

- **The Hearing Trap (Waiting to Speak):** During the meeting, Mr. Desai spent five minutes describing their business, but midway through, he mentioned a casual, non-financial detail: *"We are liquidating the subsidiary in Singapore because my daughter, who was running it, has decided to move back to our operations in Chennai."* Nandini heard the words, but she was mentally rehearsing the transition slide for the tax-neutral bond structure. She never paused to register the context.
- **The Listening Failure:** The vital piece of information was that the daughter was moving back. A true listener would have immediately paused the product talk and asked, *"How does your daughter's move to Chennai impact your succession plan? Does she need an India-domiciled trust or access to credit for the Chennai operation?"* Because Nandini was merely hearing words while waiting to

speak, she pitched a product that was structurally correct but entirely ignored the client's actual, unstated priority—their daughter's seamless transition.

The failure point was not product knowledge, but the inability to diagnose the hidden need. Nandini's focus on her own script prevented her from connecting the dots of the client's story.

The Strategic Distinction

Hearing is the minimum requirement; Listening is the strategic gateway to client needs.

Aspect	Hearing (The Passive Intake)	Listening (The Insight Lens)
Cognitive State	**Rehearsal:** Mentally preparing the next rebuttal or pitch point.	**Diagnosis:** Focusing cognitive energy solely on the client's words and body language.
Result	**Superficial:** Captures facts and surface-level data.	**Strategic:** Captures intent, hidden needs, and emotional context.
Motive	To get to **Your Turn** to deliver your planned message.	To get to **The Core Problem** so you can deliver the *right* message.
Consequence	**Transactional:** Makes the client feel ignored or rushed.	**Foundational:** Makes the client feel understood and valued.

The Strategic Analogy: The Financial Audit vs. The Forensic Audit

Hearing is the standard financial audit: it captures the numbers and facts presented on the ledger. Listening is the forensic audit: it captures the *pattern*, the *context*, and the *reason* why the numbers are presented that way. You must use your analytical skills not just on the data but on the person delivering it.

Key Takeaways & The Banker's Toolkit

Key Takeaways

- **Listening is Active, Not Passive:** It is the most demanding cognitive skill you deploy in a client meeting.
- **The 80/20 Rule of Dialogue:** In the discovery phase, the client should speak 80% of the time, and you should speak 20% (to ask clarifying questions).
- **Silence is the Banker's Best Tool:** Never interrupt. A pause, even an uncomfortable one, often encourages the client to reveal the critical, hidden detail.
- **Focus on the "Non-Financial" Details:** The strategic insight often lies in the client's casual comments about family, politics, or logistics—the things they assume you don't care about.

Quick Action Plan: The 'Active Listening Pivot'

1. **Stop the Rehearsal:** When the client is speaking, consciously stop your mind from formulating a reply. Your goal is Understanding, not Reply.
2. **Paraphrase and Validate:** After the client finishes, do not rush to pitch. Start your response by summarizing what you just heard: "*So, if I understand correctly, the daughter's move means the structure needs to be fully operational in Chennai by Q3. Is that the key constraint?*" This forces you to listen and confirms comprehension.

3. **Ask the Contextual Question:** Follow the paraphrase with a broad, open-ended question that solicits the *why*: "*How does that Q3 timeline affect your personal priorities?*"

Mental Tattoo

Hearing processes words,
Listening diagnoses needs.

CHAPTER 11

Inquiry vs. Assumption - The Hidden Cost of Guessing

THE ANCHOR

"Assumptions are the termites of relationships." — Henry Winkler

In banking, the difference between success and disaster often lies in a single, unseen detail—a small clause in a contract, an unstated familial relationship, or a non-standard covenant in existing debt. The average banker operates on Assumption, filling in knowledge gaps with guesses to save time. The strategic banker operates on Inquiry, treating every unknown as a critical piece of the puzzle that must be verified. *Assumption is the professional sin of intellectual laziness; Inquiry is the discipline of strategic precision.* Because small, unseen details hold the key to the entire mandate, the hidden cost of guessing is always catastrophic.

The Use Case Example: The Missing Covenant in Pune

Meet Karthik, a corporate lender in Pune, tasked with structuring a large term loan for TechSolve Innovations, a rapidly expanding IT consulting firm. Karthik's proposal was excellent, providing the necessary capital. During due diligence, Karthik noticed the client had substantial existing debt with a smaller, regional Credit Society.

- **The Assumption Trap:** Karthik received the standard debt summary and *assumed* the existing loan was structured with standard, market-average covenants. He assumed that because the existing loan was unsecured, it would not conflict with his new term loan. He did not explicitly inquire about the fine print of the previous loan agreement. He mentally filled in the gap: *They are a reputable company; the debt terms must be standard.* This assumption saved him three hours of legal review time.
- **The Inquiry Failure:** Three months after Karthik's loan was disbursed, TechSolve Innovations breached a seemingly minor covenant in the *old* regional loan agreement—a specific clause stating that any new financing from a national bank would trigger an immediate, unscheduled repayment demand. Because Karthik failed to inquire about the small, unseen detail, his new, larger loan instantly caused the old debt to be called, creating a liquidity crisis and damaging the client relationship beyond repair.

The failure point was that Karthik chose speed over precision. The small detail he *assumed* was standard turned out to be the single most important, deal-breaking fact.

The Strategic Distinction

Inquiry is the discipline of verification; Assumption is the reliance on unverified belief.

Aspect	Assumption (The Guessing Trap)	Inquiry (The Verification Lens)
Foundation	**Ego:** Believing you have seen this case before, leading to pattern-matching errors.	**Discipline:** Treating every client case as unique until every critical variable is verified.

Aspect	Assumption (The Guessing Trap)	Inquiry (The Verification Lens)
Motive	Driven by **Speed:** Trying to close the deal or clear the checklist faster.	Driven by **Mitigation:** Identifying the unseen risk that only precise questioning can uncover.
Focus	**The Known:** Concentrating on the facts already provided.	**The Unknown:** Concentrating on the information deliberately withheld or overlooked.
Consequence	**The Hidden Cost:** Catastrophic failure due to a single, small, unverified detail.	**The Strategic Win:** Uncovering the competitive advantage or avoiding an institutional loss.

The Strategic Analogy: The Financial Building Inspector

Assumption is like signing off on a new building because the architect's blueprint *looks* right. Inquiry is like sending a structural engineer to look at the soil, examine the unseen foundation, and verify every bolt and beam against the local code. The banker must function as a financial building inspector—you must look past the clean facade of the client's pitch to inspect the complex, unverified structure beneath.

Key Takeaways & The Banker's Toolkit

Key Takeaways

- **Assume Nothing, Verify Everything:** The bank is paying you to verify the assumptions of the client, not to adopt them.
- **The "Small Detail" Test:** The more standard or generic a document or detail appears (e.g., "standard debt

covenants"), the more ruthlessly you must inquire about its precise language.

- **The Three Most Dangerous Assumptions:** Never assume *standard debt covenants, consistent family relationships* in HNI succession, or *stable regulatory frameworks* in emerging markets.
- **Ask the Negative Question:** Don't just ask, *"Do we have permission?"* Ask, *"Is there any clause in any existing agreement that explicitly forbids this new transaction?"*

Quick Action Plan: The 'Verification Loop'

1. **Map the Gaps:** Review the client pitch or legal document and identify every point where you used a general knowledge phrase (e.g., "standard terms," "market rate," "typical arrangement").
2. **Translate to Inquiry:** Convert each gap into a specific, closed-ended question requiring a definitive document or answer (e.g., Change *"Are your covenants okay?"* to *"Please provide the full text of Section 4.C detailing acceleration clauses in the event of new debt issuance"*.
3. **Validate the Unseen:** If the client provides a summary, insist on the source document. The strategic value is in the primary source, not the client's interpretation.

Mental Tattoo

Assumption is unpriced risk,
Inquiry is due diligence.

CHAPTER 12

Empathy vs. Sympathy - The Difference Between Feeling and Doing

---

THE ANCHOR

"Sympathy listens to pain. Empathy takes responsibility for its resolution." — Author

---

The financial services professional is constantly navigating human stress and corporate urgency. This makes Empathy a non-negotiable skill. Yet, the vast majority of bankers fail to master it because they stop short, mistaking mere sympathy for the required level of action. This error costs not only relationships but also revenue. The difference is the strategic pivot: moving from feeling for the client's pain to diagnosing their problem and providing a *financial prescription.*

The Use Case Example: The Treasury Sales Call in Bengaluru

Meet Priya, a seasoned Treasury Sales Manager in Bengaluru, who was managing the working capital needs of TechNova Solutions, a high-growth technology start-up. The Finance Head, Suman, was clearly overwhelmed and called Priya complaining about the high cost and complexity of their current payment system, which was frustrating her team.

- **The Sympathy Trap:** Priya, hearing Suman's emotional exhaustion, spent fifteen minutes offering condolences. *"I know how stressful it is when your payment rails fail.*

I'm sorry you're having to deal with this." While the connection felt genuine, Priya's response was passive. She acknowledged the feeling, but did not address the root cause, allowing Suman to remain stuck in the problem.

- **The Empathy Solution:** A highly effective banker in Priya's position recognizes that the emotional drain is merely a symptom of a structural failure in their cash management. The solution is not comfort, but clarity. The empathic response would pivot: *"I understand the frustration. Let's translate this into a measurable problem. If we can centralize your payment reconciliation through a new API, what is the exact amount of labor hours and bank fees we can cut? I can present a solution that moves you from frustration to immediate cost savings."*

TechNova Solutions ended up engaging with the competitor who presented a Cash Management System upgrade. The competitor's success was not due to a better relationship, but a superior application of empathy: they translated emotional pain into a financially quantifiable problem they could immediately solve.

The failure occurs at the moment the banker confuses emotional validation with professional responsibility. When Priya stopped at sympathy—acknowledging stress without diagnosing its cause—she unintentionally froze the client inside the problem. What felt humane in the moment became commercially negligent. This is where most bankers lose relevance: they listen to pain but fail to translate it into a solvable, financial variable. Sympathy soothes emotions; it does not reduce costs, eliminate complexity, or restore control. The competitor won not by caring more, but by converting emotion into diagnosis and action. In financial services, the client does not reward the banker who understands the pain—they reward the one who removes it.

The Strategic Distinction

The core difference is that sympathy is a passive sentiment, whereas empathy in banking is an active, strategic diagnostic.

Aspect	Sympathy (The Trap)	Empathy (The Problem-Solving Lens)
Core Action	Feeling *for* the client (pity, sorrow, condolences).	Feeling *with* the client (understanding their perspective and position).
Focus	The client's **emotion** (the stress, the frustration).	The client's **structural problem** (the technical failure, the cost leak).
Outcome	Emotional validation; no commercial outcome.	Diagnosis → Product Prescription → Revenue

The Strategic Analogy: The Financial Doctor

The banker is a financial doctor. The *Sympathetic Banker* is a friend who says, *"I'm sorry you feel sick."* The *Empathic Banker* is the clinician who says, *"I understand your pain. Now let's run the tests and prescribe the right medicine."* You utilize your product suite (credit, treasury, FX, etc.) as the cure for the client's pain, but you only know which cure to apply when you exercise true empathy to find the root illness.

Key Takeaways & The Banker's Toolkit

Key Takeaways

- **Empathy is the foundation of consultative selling:** It is the required step *before* offering any product.
- The only way to move beyond sympathy is to immediately translate the client's emotional complaint into a *quantifiable business metric* (cost, risk, time, or complexity).

- If you leave a client meeting and they feel better but haven't discussed a solution, you stopped at sympathy. *Empathy is demonstrated through your strategic follow-up action.*
- A client expects their banker to be a *problem solver, not a therapist.*

Quick Action Plan: The 'Emotion-to-Action' Pivot

1. **Acknowledge (Sympathy):** Start with an empathic phrase like, "*That sounds incredibly complex and frustrating.*"
2. **Diagnose (Empathy):** Immediately pivot to diagnosis: *"What is the measurable impact of this on your Q4 operating budget?"*
3. **Prescribe (Solution):** Offer a product-agnostic solution: *"We need a structural fix that simplifies your Treasury operations." (Then follow up with the specific product recommendation.)*

Mental Tattoo

Sympathy feels the problem,
Empathy Prevents the next one.

CHAPTER 13

Trust vs. Credibility - The Difference Between Being Believed and Being Chosen

---

THE ANCHOR

"Credibility is based on results. Trust is based on intentions."
— Stephen M.R. Covey

In financial services, professionals often confuse the two primary pillars of client belief: Credibility and Trust. Credibility is a quantitative, easily proven asset—it's based on your bank's published performance metrics, its credit rating, and the branch's deposit size. It gets you an audience. Trust is a qualitative, emotional asset—it's based on the client's belief in your character, your intentions, and your unwavering commitment to their best interest. The strategic banker understands that Credibility earns belief, but Trust earns the mandate and guarantees loyalty during a crisis.

The Use Case Example: The Branch Manager's Reputation in Mumbai

Meet Sanjay, the highly effective Branch Manager of a major national bank in Mumbai. His branch was a beacon of Credibility: it had the highest deposit growth in the region, lowest asset non-performance, and the bank had just won a prestigious industry award.

- **High Credibility:** A new, high-net-worth client, Mr. Vinay Sharma, approached Sanjay's branch because of these publicly Credible facts. He was ready to move his business, convinced by the bank's stellar reputation.
- **The Trust Test:** Two months later, the parent bank faced a sudden, widely publicized reputational crisis due to a major trading loss in its international division. The news was sensational, causing some account holders to panic. Despite the branch's strong local performance, the bank's system-wide Credibility was temporarily damaged. Mr. Sharma, the new client, called Sanjay, worried. Sanjay did not try to lie or downplay the international loss (that would damage credibility). Instead, he told Mr. Sharma: *"Mr. Sharma, the news is accurate, but I want you to look at my team and me. We have managed your local portfolio with zero loss, and my personal commitment to you has not changed. I will personally monitor your liquidity."*
- **The Outcome:** Mr. Sharma stayed. He later explained that while the bank's Credibility was shaken, his Trust in Sanjay—the person he knew and whose local reputation he relied on—was solid. The relationship survived the systemic crisis because Sanjay had prioritized building a personal trust relationship over relying purely on the bank's institutional credibility.

The failure point would have been Sanjay arguing only the facts. Instead, he successfully pivoted from *institutional Credibility (which was damaged) to personal Trust (which was intact).*

The Strategic Distinction

Credibility is earned with data and past results; Trust is earned with consistent character and proven intention.

Aspect	Credibility (The Logical Pillar)	Trust (The Character Pillar)
Foundation	**External Facts:** Bank ratings, track record, branch deposit size, awards.	**Internal Character:** Honesty, reliability, proven self-sacrifice (putting client first).
Acquisition	**Demonstration:** Achieved quickly by showing evidence.	**Time & Behavior:** Achieved slowly through consistent, ethical, non-monetized actions.
Function	Gets you **an Audience** and justifies your fee.	Gets you **the Mandate** and ensures client loyalty during crises.
Risk	Can be **Lost Quickly** by one factual error or market downturn.	**Endures Market Volatility** because it is based on character, not performance.

The Strategic Analogy: The Financial Tool and the Navigator

Credibility is the high-powered, perfectly accurate analytical tool (a financial model). Trust is the seasoned navigator who has guided you through countless storms and never steered you wrong. The client needs the tool, but they choose the navigator.

Key Takeaways & The Banker's Toolkit

Key Takeaways

- **Trust is the highest-margin asset you own:** It allows you to survive institutional or market crises where credibility alone would fail.
- **The Crisis Call:** The true test of your trust account is what you say and do when there is *zero* personal or institutional upside for you.

- **The Branch Manager's Moat:** Your local, personal reputation (Trust) is your only defense when the parent institution's reputation (Credibility) is attacked.
- **Focus on Intention:** When credibility is low, pivot the conversation away from results and toward your personal process and unwavering commitment to the client's long-term welfare.

Quick Action Plan: The 'Trust Building Audit'

1. **Map the Non-Revenue Interactions:** Identify two regular interactions with the client that have *zero potential revenue* attached (e.g., a simple market insight email, an introduction to a non-bank vendor).
2. **Execute the Trust Signal:** Prioritize these non-revenue-generating interactions. They are low-cost, high-return signals that your motive is partnership, not transaction.
3. **The Crisis Rehearsal:** Mentally rehearse the key phrase you would use if the bank faced a crisis. Ensure it focuses 100% on their stability and 0% on your product portfolio.

Mental Tattoo

Credibility is proven in good times,
Trust is proven in bad ones.

CHAPTER 14

Clarity vs. Jargon - The Difference Between Communicating and Confusing

THE ANCHOR

"The ability to simplify means to eliminate the unnecessary so that the necessary may speak". — Hans Hofmann.

In the financial world, expertise is non-negotiable, but how that expertise is conveyed is the ultimate test of a banker's professionalism. Clarity ensures the client makes an informed decision; jargon—the use of specialized, unnecessarily complex, or internal terminology—only serves the banker's ego. The distinction is simple: Clarity builds trust; jargon builds a wall. Never forget: the client's decision-making process stops the moment they feel too confused or intimidated to ask a follow-up question.

The Use Case Example: The Confused Corporate Client in Delhi

Meet Geetha, a promising corporate banker in Delhi, pitching a specialized Term Loan restructuring to Pioneer Logistics, a medium-sized firm expanding its fleet. Geetha wanted to impress the owner, Mr. Thomas Varghese, with her deep understanding of the bank's internal processes.

- **The Jargon Trap:** Geetha's proposal discussion was littered with internal banking jargon and business (financial) acronyms: *"We are structuring this as an NCD to ensure better ALM fit, but our Credit Review Committee (CRC) will require a lower DSCR due to the high LTV of the rolling stock."* Mr. Varghese, the owner, was concerned with cash flow and interest rates, not internal bank acronyms. He was unfamiliar with terms *like ALM (Asset-Liability Management) and DSCR (Debt Service Coverage Ratio).* He listened passively, nodding occasionally. He perceived the complex language not as a sign of expertise, but as a deliberate attempt to conceal complexity or, worse, obfuscate hidden risks.

- **The Lost Opportunity:** The deal stalled. Mr. Varghese later told his existing banker that the proposal sounded *"too complicated" and that the competitor "spoke clearly."* The competitor had won, not because of a better rate, but because they used simple terms: *"This is a secured business loan; we just need to ensure your company's profits (DSCR) cover the repayment comfortably."* Geetha used her knowledge as a barrier to impress;

the competitor used their knowledge as a bridge to empower.

The failure point occurred the moment Geetha confused complexity with competence. When Mr. Varghese stopped asking questions and began nodding, the decision process had already shut down. Passive agreement was mistaken for understanding. By using internal jargon, she shifted the conversation from the client's needs to her own expertise, placing herself on the bank's side of the table. The competitor won by translating, not impressing—making the client feel informed and in control. Most deals are lost not through rejection, but through confusion disguised as consent.

The Strategic Distinction

Clarity is a commitment to the client's comprehension; jargon is a commitment to the banker's ego.

Aspect	Jargon (The Barrier)	Clarity (The Translation way)
Foundation	**Ego/Insecurity:** Hiding simple ideas behind complex words to sound smarter.	**Mastery:** Using simple language to explain complex ideas (The ultimate display of confidence).
Communication	**Verbal Shorthand:** Using internal acronyms (e.g., LTV, RoE, NPA).	**Analogies:** Using relatable, real-world comparisons (e.g., Insurance policy, a balance sheet as a photograph).

Aspect	Jargon (The Barrier)	Clarity (The Translation way)
Client Perception	**Intimidating** and **Suspect** (They doubt the banker's honesty).	**Empowering** and **Trustworthy** (They feel in control).
Goal	To create **distance** and **superiority**.	To establish **shared understanding** and **trust**.

The Strategic Analogy: The Financial Translator

The banker is a financial translator. You stand between the complex, acronym-laden world of internal systems and the client's desire for simple, actionable insights. Jargon forces the client to learn your language; Clarity delivers the message in *the client's language*. Never use a technical term if a plain one will suffice, and if you must use one, immediately follow it with a common analogy.

Key Takeaways & The Banker's Toolkit

Key Takeaways

- **Jargon is Arrogance in Disguise:** Always suspect your own use of technical terms. If you sound smart, but the client doesn't fully grasp the concept, you have failed.
- **The Grandma Rule:** Before using any term, mentally ask yourself, *"Could I explain this concept to my grandmother?"* If the answer is no, simplify.
- **The "What It Does" Principle:** Focus less on *what* the product is (e.g., "Non-Convertible Debenture") and more on *what* it does for the client (e.g., "A secured loan that provides stable, fixed income").

- **Never Use Internal Acronyms** with a client unless it's a common industry term (e.g., EBITDA), and always confirm their understanding first.

Quick Action Plan: The 'Jargon Filter'

1. **Prep Time:** Before the meeting, identify 3-5 technical terms you are most likely to use, and prepare a one-sentence, non-financial analogy for each.
2. **Confirmation Check:** After using any unavoidable technical term, immediately pause and ask a confirmation question: *"Does that 'DSCR' concept make sense, or should I rephrase it in terms of how much profit you need to comfortably pay the loan?"*
3. **Client Language Mirror:** Listen for the terminology the client uses. When replying, mirror their simpler language rather than imposing your complex terms.

Mental Tattoo

Jargon impresses peers,
Clarity earns clients.

CHAPTER 15

Verbal vs. Non-Verbal Communication - The Banker's Body Language in High-Stakes Deals

---

THE ANCHOR

"People may hear your words, but they feel your attitude."
— John C. Maxwell

In high-stakes financial services, the Verbal message—the pitch, the numbers, the product details—is only a fraction of the conversation. The rest is conveyed through Non-Verbal Communication: eye contact, posture, gestures, and tone. The strategic banker understands that the non-verbal message is the editor of the verbal message. If your verbal message projects confidence but your body language betrays anxiety (e.g., fidgeting or poor posture), the client will always believe the non-verbal signal. Mastering the control of your physical presence is the ultimate act of professional composure.

The Use Case Example: The Shaky Pitch in Ahmedabad

Meet Sarita, a highly competent M&A Associate in Ahmedabad, pitching a complex corporate restructuring to Apex Industries. Her Verbal presentation was flawlessly structured: the valuation was correct, and the synergies were clearly modeled.

- **The Non-Verbal Trap:** During the Q&A, the CEO of Apex Industries asked a pointed question about the timing of debt issuance. Sarita knew the answer, and she delivered the correct, confident verbal response. However, under pressure, she: *1) Fidgeted* with her pen, *2) Slightly hunched* her shoulders, and *3) Broke eye contact* with the CEO for a crucial five seconds while she spoke.
- **The Client Perception:** The client wasn't primarily focused on the Verbal answer (the facts). They were assessing Sarita's composure under stress. The CEO interpreted her fidgeting and broken eye contact as a lack of confidence in the underlying facts, a sign of intellectual insecurity, or even a hidden risk. The CEO later commented that while the numbers were right, the presentation *"felt shaky."* The deal stalled, not on analysis, but on the perceived emotional stability of the advisor.

The failure point was the disconnect between the two channels. Sarita's anxious body language edited her verbal message from *"I know the answer" to "I am unsure, but I am saying the answer."*

The Strategic Distinction

Verbal communication delivers the facts; Non-Verbal communication delivers the conviction.

Aspect	Verbal Communication (The Facts)	Non-Verbal Communication (The Conviction)
Foundation	**Words, Data, Numbers,** and **Formal Language.**	**Posture, Eye Contact, Tone,** and **Gestures.**
Function	**Informs** the client (Tells them *what*).	**Persuades** the client (Tells them *why* they should believe you).

Aspect	Verbal Communication (The Facts)	Non-Verbal Communication (The Conviction)
Control	Highly conscious and easily rehearsed.	Often subconscious and betrayed by stress.
Client Priority	The client evaluates accuracy and logic	The client evaluates confidence, credibility, and risk comfort.

The Strategic Analogy: The Financial Ledger and the Signature

Verbal communication is the financial ledger: it contains all the figures, the income, and the expenses. Non-Verbal communication is the signature on the document—it validates the entire transaction and confirms the commitment behind the figures. The ledger must be correct, but the client won't commit until the signature (your conviction) is assured.

Key Takeaways & The Banker's Toolkit

Key Takeaways

- **Your body speaks louder than your balance sheet:** You must manage your physical presence with the same rigor you manage your models.
- **The Non-Verbal Hierarchy:** The two most critical non-verbal signals are *Eye Contact (signals honesty and commitment)* and *Posture (signals confidence and control).*
- **Stress is Non-Verbal Fuel:** When pressure is highest (e.g., tough Q&A), your body language is most likely to betray you. This is when composure is most vital.
- **Master the Pause:** Never fidget. If you feel compelled to move, pause your speech instead. Stillness projects authority and confidence.

Quick Action Plan: The 'Composure Checklist'

1. **Anchor Your Hands:** Before a high-stakes meeting, choose a deliberate resting position for your hands (e.g., flat on the table, or lightly clasped). This eliminates fidgeting.
2. **The 3-Second Rule (Eye Contact):** When speaking, commit to maintaining eye contact with a key decision-maker for a *minimum of 3 seconds* before briefly glancing elsewhere. This signals conviction.
3. **Video Rehearsal:** Record yourself giving your most critical pitch. Mute the sound and watch only your body language. *If you look unsure on mute, your verbal pitch will fail.*

Mental Tattoo

Verbal delivers the facts,
Non-Verbal delivers the conviction.

CHAPTER 16

Assertion vs. Aggregression - The Difference Between Stating Your Position and Attacking the Client

THE ANCHOR

"Assertion protects the relationship while defending the position. Aggression sacrifices both." – Author

In banking, disagreement is a constant. Clients challenge pricing, credit officers challenge risk structures, and colleagues challenge timelines. The strategic banker must master Assertion—the ability to state one's analysis, policy, or position clearly and firmly, while maintaining respect for the counterparty. The amateur mistakes this firmness for Aggression—a hostile communication style that attacks the person rather than the problem. *Assertion preserves the relationship while winning the point; Aggression damages the relationship while only briefly claiming the win.*

The Use Case Example: The Credit Committee Showdown in Mumbai

Meet Priya, a Relationship Manager in Mumbai, presenting a challenging commercial real estate loan structure to the bank's Credit Committee. The Chief Risk Officer (CRO) challenged her valuation model, claiming her risk assumptions were too optimistic.

- **The Aggression Trap:** Priya, feeling defensive and personally attacked by the CRO's scrutiny, reacted with Aggression. She retorted: *"With all due respect, my team's model is standard; you are missing the market context, and perhaps we need to revisit the credit policy you signed off on last quarter."* She attacked the CRO's intelligence and authority. The message received was: *She is unprofessional and hostile.* The loan was denied, not because of the model's flaws, but because Priya damaged her reputation and alienated a key decision-maker.
- **The Assertion Solution:** A professional assertion would have sounded like this: *"I respect your caution on the model. My position is that the valuation is defensible because we applied a 15% discount on Q4 cash flows, exceeding the policy minimum of 10%. Let's review the policy framework together, but I am firm on this valuation."* Priya defended the Analysis (the 15% discount) without attacking the Person (the CRO's caution). She demonstrated firmness and confidence, ensuring she won intellectual respect, even if the loan required minor modification.

The failure point was misclassifying scrutiny as attack. Priya failed to separate the *professional challenge* from the *personal threat.*

The Strategic Distinction

Assertion is the method of defending your work; Aggression is the impulse to attack the challenger.

Aspect	Aggression (The Relationship Killer)	Assertion (The Boundary Lens)
Focus	**The Person:** Attacking judgment, competence, or character.	**The Problem:** Defending the facts, the policy, or the analysis.

Aspect	Aggression (The Relationship Killer)	Assertion (The Boundary Lens)
Tone	**Hostile, Defensive,** and **Emotional** (Raised voice, harsh language).	**Firm, Calm,** and **Measured** (Controlled posture, even tone).
Goal	To **Win the Fight** and defeat the counterparty.	To **Win Respect** and advance the discussion to a solution.
Consequence	Damages long-term trust and creates lasting professional animosity.	Builds credibility and establishes boundaries without burning bridges.

The Strategic Analogy: The Policy Firewall

Aggression is like shutting down the communication channel with a personal attack, preventing any resolution. Assertion is like erecting a policy firewall—it clearly defends the boundary of acceptable risk or terms (the policy) but keeps the communication lines open for the counterparty to work within those constraints. . You must assert the boundary, not destroy the bridge.

Key Takeaways & The Banker's Toolkit

Key Takeaways

- **Assertion is a defense of fact; Aggression is a defense of ego.**
- **The Key Phrase:** When challenged, always pivot from the personal to the professional: *Replace "You are wrong" with "My analysis shows a different trajectory based on the policy framework."*
- **Manage Your Physicality:** Aggression often begins with a physical change (raised voice, leaning forward). The

disciplined banker focuses on maintaining a calm, open posture (Non-Verbal control).

- **Never Use 'Always' or 'Never':** Aggressive language often uses extreme generalizations that are easy to refute. Assertion uses specific, verifiable data points.

Quick Action Plan: The 'Firmness Filter'

1. **Acknowledge First:** Before stating your assertiveness, acknowledge the other side's view to diffuse tension: *"I understand your concern about the timeline..."*
2. **State the Boundary (The "I"):** Use "I" statements to own your position without blaming the other person: *"I am unable to change the policy, as it is a mandatory regulatory requirement."*
3. **Offer the Path:** Never assert a boundary without offering a path forward: *"I am firm on the 15% discount, but I can re-model the repayment schedule to meet your comfort level."* This maintains control while offering collaboration.

Mental Tattoo

Assertion wins the point,
Aggression loses the partner.

CHAPTER 17

Response vs. Reaction – Trading Emotional impulses for Calculated decisions

THE ANCHOR

"Between stimulus and response there is a space. In that space is our power to choose our response." — Viktor Frankl

In professional life, pressure does not create mistakes—it reveals discipline. Every banker, leader, and decision-maker will face moments designed to provoke emotion: an unexpected challenge, a dismissive comment, or a public contradiction. Reaction is the instinctive, emotional reply that feels urgent but sacrifices control. Response is the deliberate, composed choice made after a conscious pause. The strategic banker understands that mastery is not proven by how quickly one speaks, but by how intentionally one chooses to speak. Creating space between stimulus and reply is not hesitation—it is authority. That pause is where judgment replaces impulse, and professionalism replaces ego.

The Use Case Example: The Conservative Growth Review in Hyderabad

Meet Vanya, a Regional Sales Head in Hyderabad, presenting her team's business plan and projected growth targets for the next fiscal year to the Executive Committee. Her projections showed a solid, but conservative, 15% growth based on current market dynamics. Midway through her review, the

Business Head cut her off and stated, *"Vanya, 15% is lazy. The competition is targeting 22%. We need to see a plan that hits 20% growth in the first year, or this plan is scrapped now."*

- **The Reaction Trap:** Vanya felt immediately attacked, believing the Business Head was questioning her effort or competence. Her mind snapped to defense. Her immediate impulse (the Reaction) was to argue, defensively justifying the 15% based on market volatility, or to impulsively promise the 20% just to survive the meeting. By reacting, she lost control of her composure and accepted the Business Head's aggressive premise, making her existing, well-researched plan look weak.
- **The Response Solution:** Vanya created the strategic pause (she took a silent breath and straightened her posture). Her Response was calm and strategic: *"Sir, I respect the challenge for 20%. Our current 15% model assumes status quo. Before I commit to 20%, I need to ask you: What specific institutional resources or strategic market actions, such as a focused acquisition or a doubling of our marketing budget, would you suggest modeling to strategically support that 20% target?"*

The Response pivoted the discussion from defending her conservative plan to inviting the Business Head to co-own the solution and share the strategic responsibility for the stretch target.

The failure point of a Reaction is that it addresses the *emotion* of the challenge; a Response addresses the *strategy* of the problem.

The Strategic Distinction

Response is the strategic choice; Reaction is the emotional impulse.

Aspect	Reaction (The Impulse)	Response (The Composure Lens)
Timing	**Immediate:** Less than one second after the stimulus; driven by the fight-or-flight instinct.	**Delayed:** Requires a deliberate, mental pause (the "Frankl Space").
Driver	**Emotion:** Fear, defensiveness, anxiety, or surprise.	**Strategy:** Policy, long-term goal, or a pre-planned answer.
Outcome	**Escalation:** Confirms the challenger's premise and increases tension.	**De-escalation:** Takes control of the tone and reframes the problem.
Body Language	**Tense:** Raised voice, flushed face, tense posture.	**Composed:** Even tone, maintained eye contact, relaxed posture.

The Strategic Analogy: The Financial Circuit Breaker

Reaction is like a power surge hitting a financial circuit board—it causes an immediate, uncontrolled explosion and forces a system shutdown. Response is like a well-calibrated circuit breaker—it deliberately creates a millisecond of pause to assess the surge and strategically reroutes power to prevent damage. The disciplined banker installs a mental circuit breaker to protect their professional composure.

Key Takeaways & The Banker's Toolkit

Key Takeaways

- **The Power is in the Pause:** The most important thing you do after a challenge is often nothing—a silent breath is your most powerful strategic move.
- **Response Reframes; Reaction Justifies.** Your goal is not to prove you were right (Reaction), but to reframe

the problem into a controllable, collaborative solution (Response).

- **The Strategic Pivot:** When a number is challenged, pivot the conversation immediately from the *result* (the 15% target) to the *inputs* and *resources* (the strategic investment required to hit 20%).
- **The Anticipatory Rehearsal:** Mentally rehearse the three toughest questions you might face and how you will initiate your pause before giving your answer.

Quick Action Plan: The '3-Second Circuit Breaker'

1. **Stop Signal:** When a challenging question hits, force yourself to physically stop all motion (don't nod, don't move your hands).
2. **The Anchor (The Pause):** Engage the *3-Second Circuit Breaker* by taking one deep, silent breath or taking a deliberate sip of water. This creates the essential space between stimulus and reply.
3. **Execute the Reframing:** Use the time gained to pivot the conversation: *"That's an excellent challenge. To address that strategically, I need to ask..."* This redirects the focus from confrontation to collaboration.

Mental Tattoo

Reaction escalates,
Response controls.

CHAPTER 18

Feedback vs. Criticism - The Art of Driving Performance Not Demoralization

THE ANCHOR

"Feedback is the breakfast of champions."— Ken Blanchard

In the professional world, the exchange of insights is necessary for improvement. However, the effectiveness of that exchange depends entirely on its structure: Feedback is a strategic tool for improvement; Criticism is a destructive commentary on character. *Feedback is about correction; Criticism is about condemnation.* This distinction defines leadership: great managers offer feedback to build a better future process, while poor leaders resort to criticism to tear down past effort. Your ability to deliver structured, future-focused advice during a review determines whether you motivate a colleague or merely demoralize them.

The Use Case Example: The Mid-Year Review in Ahmedabad

Meet Nisha, a seasoned Portfolio Manager in Ahmedabad, conducting the mid-year performance review with her junior Credit Analyst, Harsha. Harsha excelled at complex modeling (IQ) but consistently struggled with the soft skill of client communication, often causing minor relationship friction. This was the focus of the review.

- **The Criticism Trap:** Nisha, frustrated that the issue had surfaced again, began the review with a broad judgment:

  "Harsha, client communication continues to be a weakness for you. It's affecting how clients perceive us, and it raises concerns about your readiness for greater responsibility."

  While not intentionally harsh, the feedback focused on Harsha's perceived limitations as a professional, rather than on a specific, correctable behavior. Harsha internalized the message as a fixed personal flaw, became defensive, and disengaged from the discussion.

- **The Feedback Solution:** A more effective approach would have been structured and specific:

  "Harsha, let's review the last three client calls. In the TechSolutions discussion, you interrupted the client twice while they were explaining their constraints. That interruption caused the negotiation to stall. This is a process issue we can fix. In the next call, I want you to consciously apply the Active Listening Pivot—pause, summarize the client's point, and then respond. Let's review how that changes the outcome."

  This reframed the issue from who Harsha is to what Harsha can do differently, converting defensiveness into ownership and improvement.

The failure point was that Nisha focused on who (Harsha's permanent flaw) rather than what (the measurable communication action) and how (the future training solution). Criticism generates emotional defence; Feedback generates actionable change.

The Strategic Distinction

Feedback is a systematic evaluation of an action; criticism is a subjective judgment of a person.

Aspect	Criticism (The Demoralizer)	Feedback (The Performance lens)
Focus	**The Person:** Character, personality, or perceived effort ("You are disorganized").	**The Action:** Measurable behavior or task outcome ("The report was late").
Direction	**The Past:** Focuses on failure that cannot be undone.	**The Future:** Focuses on actionable steps for improvement.
Motive	Driven by **Frustration/ Judgment** (The manager's feeling).	Driven by **Improvement/ Correction** (The necessary business outcome).
Impact	**Erodes Trust:** Causes defensiveness and resentment.	**Builds Trust:** Provides a path to success.

The Strategic Analogy: The Financial Model Debugger

In banking, your service is often built on complex financial models. Criticism is yelling at the model developer for being "incompetent" because of the error. Feedback is pointing exactly to the incorrect cell in the spreadsheet, explaining *why* the formula is flawed, and then collaboratively building a more robust formula for the next iteration. Feedback isolates the flaw to correct the system, not the person.

Key Takeaways & The Banker's Toolkit

Key Takeaways

- **Criticism is destructive; Feedback is architectural:** Always aim to build a better future process, not tear down past effort.
- **The Golden Rule:** Always start with the measurable positive outcome before introducing the necessary correction. This grounds the conversation in success, not failure.
- **Be Specific:** Never use sweeping generalizations like "always" or "never." Feedback must be specific to the last task (e.g., "The formatting in the Q3 presentation was inconsistent").
- **Feedback is Collaborative:** End every feedback session by asking, "What resources do *you* need from me to ensure this goes smoothly next time?"

Quick Action Plan: The 'Situational Feedback' Model

1. **Situation:** Describe the exact, objective behavior or action that occurred. (e.g., "The Q3 report was delivered three days after the deadline.")
2. **Impact:** Describe the measurable, objective consequence. (e.g., "This delayed our presentation to the committee and required me to adjust the data under pressure.")
3. **Next Step:** Define the specific, mutually agreed-upon solution for the future. (e.g., "Moving forward, let's schedule a draft review 7 days before the final deadline.")

Mental Tattoo

Criticism judges,
Feedback improves.

CHAPTER 19

Curiosity vs. Interrogation - Navigating Due Diligence with Diplomacy

THE ANCHOR

"Curiosity invites understanding whereas interrogation invites defense". — Author

---

The foundation of the lending process is curiosity—the professional need to ask every necessary question to understand the client's financial position and risk profile. However, when the client feels the banker is starting from a position of suspicion rather than partnership, that curiosity quickly mutates into interrogation. This distinction is critical: Curiosity seeks clarity to approve the loan; interrogation seeks faults to reject it. Your ability to maintain a tone of partnership, even when asking tough questions, determines whether the client feels valued or scrutinized.

The Use Case Example: The Corporate Loan Review in Chennai

Meet Karthik, a corporate relationship manager in Chennai, tasked with obtaining a crucial sanction for a ₹50 Crore expansion loan for AgriGro Exports, a large agribusiness client. During the due diligence process, the bank's credit risk team flagged a recent, non-recurring write-off in the company's accounts and demanded a follow-up.

- **The Interrogation Trap:** Karthik, fearing the risk team's disapproval, adopted their defensive posture. In his meeting with the Finance Director, he fired off rapid-fire questions: *"Was this a deliberate concealment? Why was this not flagged immediately? Who exactly signed off on this write-off?"* Karthik failed to provide context or empathy. He was transmitting the internal suspicion of the risk department directly to the client. The client immediately became defensive, perceiving the banker as an auditor sent to find fraud, not a partner trying to close the loan. The client reluctantly provided the documents but began exploring options with another bank.
- **The Curiosity Solution:** A skilled banker uses curiosity to bridge the gap. They would frame the question: *"To get this loan approved, we need to show our risk team we fully understand this transaction. Could you help us explain the strategic context of this write-off so we can present a clean, strong case for approval?"*

The failure point was tone and motive. Karthik's questions were transactional and accusatory, turning a necessary clarification into a breakdown of trust.

The Strategic Distinction

Curiosity is a tool for partnership and mitigation; interrogation is a barrier built on suspicion and judgment.

Aspect	Interrogation (The Barrier)	Curiosity (The Partnership lens)
Motive	Driven by **fear of failure** (The banker's fear of the risk team).	Driven by **desire for accuracy** (The need for complete data).
Tone	**Accusatory** and **Judgmental** ("Why did you do X?").	**Collaborative** and **Neutral** ("Help us understand X").
Communication	Closed-ended questions leading to "yes/no" answers.	Open-ended questions seeking **context** and **strategy**.
Client Perception	**Threatening:** The banker is a gatekeeper.	**Partnering:** The banker is an advocate.

The Strategic Analogy: The Shared Blueprint

In lending, the banker and the client are reading a complex financial blueprint. Interrogation is accusing the client of hiding lines on the blueprint. Curiosity is saying, *"Our internal team has a question about this specific line item; can we clarify it so the construction (the loan) can proceed?"* Curiosity frames the tough question as a necessary step for *mutual success.*

Key Takeaways & The Banker's Toolkit

Key Takeaways

- **The Advocate Mindset:** When asking tough questions, remember you are the client's advocate to the risk team. Frame the question as seeking information for the client, not against them.

- **Context is King:** Never ask a "what" question ("What happened to this fund?"). Always ask a "why" or "how" question ("How does this decision fit into your long-term growth strategy?").
- **The Question Sandwich:** Always preface a tough question with a statement of validation, and conclude it with a statement of partnership (e.g., "We appreciate your transparency... [Tough Question]... this detail will help me secure the final approval.")
- **Source of the Question:** Be transparent. Say, "*The credit team needs clarification on...*" rather than making the question sound like your personal doubt.

Quick Action Plan: The 'Contextual Query'

1. **Frame the Need:** State the reason for the question *before* asking it: *"To efficiently manage the loan approval timeline, we need to clarify..."*
2. **Soften the Query:** Substitute judgmental words (e.g., "error," "issue") with neutral terms like *"context," "rationale," or "strategic fit."*
3. **Define the Outcome:** End the tough questioning by reiterating the positive outcome: "*Thank you, this context is exactly what we need to move the sanction forward.*"

Mental Tattoo

Curiosity explores,
Interrogation accuses.

PART III:
The Action - Salesmanship & Strategic Relationship Mastery

The Pivot from Execution to Endurance

If *Part I (The Mindset)* built your internal architecture and *Part II (The Dialogue)* refined how you engage with clients, *Part III is where those capabilities are translated into sustainable commercial outcomes.* This section addresses the defining challenge of modern banking: *the shift from transactional selling to strategic advising.*

Revenue, at the highest level of banking, is not extracted through persuasion alone. It is earned through judgment, trust, relevance, and long-term alignment. Strategy, therefore, is not about products or pricing—it is about understanding human psychology, managing risk over time, and becoming essential to the client's decision-making process.

These distinctions separate *high-activity performers* from *high-impact bankers*—the difference between being a replaceable vendor and becoming a trusted, long-term partner.

Your Progression Through Part III

This section is structured to reflect the strategic sales process, moving from foundational positioning to execution tactics and finally, long-term retention:

1. **Foundational Positioning (Selling & Value):** We start by dissecting the core strategic choice: adopting the posture of an Advisor who delivers Value rather than a Seller who pushes Price.

2. **Strategic Diagnosis (Need & Wealth):** We then sharpen your diagnostic skills to uncover the client's true Need and apply sophistication (differentiating Rich vs. Wealthy) to ensure alignment.

3. **Execution Tactics (Upselling, Personalisation & Persuasion):** This section refines your closing skills, focusing on tactics for growth (Cross-Selling vs. Up-

Selling), client experience (Personalisation), and ethical closure (Persuasion).

4. **Relationship Mastery (Loyalty & Customer experience):** We conclude with the mastery of time and commitment, ensuring your dedication translates to strategic client retention (Loyalty) and effective customer experience.

Mastering Part III is not about outperforming a quarter. It is about earning the right to be consulted before decisions are made—and building a career defined not by volume, but by relevance and durability.

No.	Core Distinction	The Strategic Progression
20.	Selling vs. Advising	The core strategic shift: positioning yourself as a problem solver, not a product pusher.
21.	Price vs. Value	Justifying your solution so cost becomes irrelevant after the advisory relationship is established.
22.	Rich vs. Wealthy	Foundational concept for segmenting and advising HNI and Ultra HNI clients.
23.	Standardisation vs Tailoring	Tailoring product delivery versus bespoke product design.
24.	Customer Service vs. Customer Experience	Tactical error fixing and managing the client's entire journey with the bank.
25.	Cross-Selling vs. Up-Selling	The tactics of maximizing wallet share - Breadth versus Depth.

No.	Core Distinction	The Strategic Progression
26.	Networking vs. Socialism	The practical application of managing professional connections versus personal time.
27 .	Loyalty vs. Satisfaction	The ultimate retention metric: engineered dependency or fleeting happiness.
28 .	Persuasion vs. Manipulation	The final boundary- defining the ethical limits of sales influence.

CHAPTER 20

Selling vs. Advising - The Core Shift from Vendor to Partner

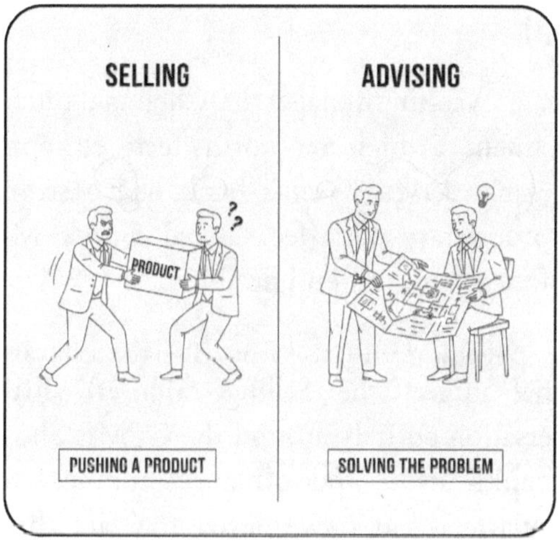

THE ANCHOR

"The purpose of a business is to create a customer."— Peter Drucker

---

In financial services, professionals face a binary choice every day: to function as a Seller or as an Advisor. Selling is a transactional, product-centric approach focused on immediate execution and near-term outcomes and targets. Advising is a strategic, client-centric approach focused on achieving the client's long-term objectives, even if it means sacrificing an immediate fee. The strategic banker understands that selling is about closing the deal; advising is about opening the relationship. The shift from vendor to partner is the single most important strategic decision a modern banker can make.

The Use Case Example: The Mutual Fund Pitch in Chennai

Meet Geeta, a Wealth Manager in Chennai, pitching to Mr. Sudhir Krishnan, a high-net-worth tech entrepreneur with significant cash reserves. Geeta's bank had a strong mandate to push a proprietary, high-fee Global Equity Mutual Fund (GEMF) before the month-end deadline.

- **The Selling Trap:** Geeta, focused on her personal internal target (the Selling mindset), structured the conversation entirely around the GEMF. She emphasized the bank's strong performance numbers for the last two quarters and downplayed the fact that the client was already over-exposed to global equity markets. She anchored the discussion around a solution that aligned with internal priorities rather than Mr. Krishnan's risk profile. As a result, the conversation felt standardized, and Mr. Krishnan perceived the engagement as transactional rather than tailored.

- **The Advising Solution:** An Advisor would have begun with strategic diagnosis. They would have listened (as defined in Part II) to discover that Mr. Krishnan's primary concern was capital preservation and diversification due to an upcoming international expansion. The Advisor would have opened with: *"Given your expansion, the strategic move is a low-risk, liquidity-focused Treasury structure, not a high-risk equity fund."*

Even if the treasury product carried a lower immediate fee, the Advisor built indelible Trust by prioritizing client needs over bank targets.

The failure point was that Geeta saw a wallet to fill; the Advisor saw a complex risk profile to manage. The Advisor ensured the client would call them first for the next, much larger mandate.

The Strategic Distinction

Selling is product-focused and transactional; Advising is client-focused and relational.

Aspect	Selling (The Transactional Mindset)	Advising (The Strategic Banker's Way)
Focus	**Product & Fee:** What the bank needs to move; the size of the immediate commission.	**Client Outcome & Risk:** What the client needs to achieve; the integrity of the solution.
Motive	Driven by **The Target:** Quarterly numbers and internal deadlines.	Driven by **The Diagnosis:** Uncovering and solving the root cause of the client's financial pain.
Communication	**Telling:** Presenting facts, features, and benefits.	**Asking:** Inquiry, diagnosis, and validating the client's unstated concerns.
Relationship Term	**Short-Term:** Focus on the single, fast closure.	**Long-Term:** Focus on the client's lifetime value and referral potential.

The Strategic Analogy: The Navigator vs. The Vendor

Selling is acting as a vendor—efficiently offering a product based on what is requested. Advising is acting as a navigator—first understanding the destination, the risks along the route, and the client's tolerance for uncertainty, before recommending the best path forward. The product matters, but the route matters more. Clients don't need more vendors; they need navigators who can guide them through complexity with judgment and foresight.

Key Takeaways & The Banker's Toolkit

Key Takeaways

- **Your Revenue is a By-product of Your Advice:** The highest fees are earned when the client perceives you as a strategic partner, not a sales pitch.
- **The Strategic Pause:** Before presenting any product, create a non-monetized dialogue pause dedicated solely to confirming the client's risk profile and long-term goals.
- **Be Prepared to Say No:** The single best advisory tool is the ability to tell the client not to buy the specific product your bank is pushing, if it conflicts with their interest.
- **Sell the Problem, Not the Product:** Focus your pitch 80% on validating the client's pain point and 20% on how your product solves it.

Quick Action Plan: The 'Advisor's Pivot'

1. **Stop the Pitch:** If you feel you are pushing a product, stop the conversation immediately.

2. **Verify the Need:** Ask the client: *"Based on what I've heard, I believe your primary Need is [X risk mitigation]. Is that accurate, or is your primary Want something different?"*

3. **Recommend the Strategy (Not the Product):** Pivot from pitching the GEMF to recommending the Strategy (e.g., "The optimal strategy now is capital preservation via low-risk instruments"). Only after they agree to the strategy do you introduce the product.

Mental Tattoo

**Selling moves the product,
Advising moves the client.**

CHAPTER 21

Price vs. Value - The Language of Justification

THE ANCHOR

"Price is what you pay. Value is what you get." — Warren Buffett

---

In every client interaction, the banker is asked, directly or indirectly, to justify the cost of their service. Price is a simple, quantifiable number—the interest rate, the commission, the fee. It is easily compared and often commoditized. Value is the total benefit delivered: the strategic insight, the risk mitigated, the peace of mind, and the access to deep expertise. The strategic banker never competes on Price; they anchor the conversation on Value. The goal is to make the client perceive your higher price as a non-negotiable investment in a superior outcome.

The Use Case Example: The Trade Finance Guarantee in Mumbai

Meet Rohan, a Trade Finance specialist in Mumbai, pitching a complex Letter of Credit (LC) facility to UniChem Exports. The facility was crucial for a new, high-volume shipping contract. The client's procurement head informed Rohan that a rival bank had offered a Price that was 15% lower in fees and 50 basis points tighter on the spread.

- **The Price Trap:** Rohan briefly considered the most common—and most dangerous—response: engaging on price. He could have defended his fee, offered a tactical concession, or attempted to "match the market" to keep the conversation alive. This is the moment where many bankers unintentionally surrender control. By allowing the discussion to be framed as a comparison of basis points and percentages, the banker reduces a complex risk solution into a commodity. In that frame, every bank looks interchangeable, differentiation collapses, and the only lever left is margin erosion. The client, meanwhile, evaluates the decision as a procurement exercise rather than a risk decision—optimizing for short-term savings instead of long-term certainty.

- **The Value Solution:** Rohan refused to compete on price. He reframed the conversation immediately. He asserted: *"We are 15% more expensive because we are selling you certainty, not just capital. Our fee covers our dedicated, in-house compliance team and our guaranteed 24-hour document turnaround. The cheaper price means they outsource this to a vendor. If their documentation is delayed or has a single error, your shipment is stalled, leading to a multi-lakh penalty and a damaged reputation with your buyer. Our higher Price is your lowest Risk premium."*

The failure point would have been negotiating the fee. Rohan succeeded because he shifted the client's focus from the transactional cost (Price) to the non-quantifiable, existential benefit (avoidance of supply chain risk and reputational damage—Value).

The Strategic Distinction

Price is the cost of the transaction; Value is the worth of the outcome.

Aspect	Price (The Commodity)	Value (The Strategic Asset)
Quantification	**Measurable:** Numerical, comparative, and easily benchmarked (e.g., basis points, fee percentage).	**Qualitative:** Non-numerical, based on emotional and strategic outcomes (e.g., peace of mind, guaranteed security).
Focus	**Cost:** What the client loses (money).	**Benefit:** What the client gains (risk mitigation, time saved, future opportunity).
Language	**Defensive:** Justifying the cost against competitors.	**Assertive:** Defining the cost as a necessary investment in the outcome.
Strategy	To be the cheapest option.	To be the safest, most comprehensive option.

The Strategic Analogy: The Financial Parachute

Price is the cost of buying a parachute. Value is the guarantee that the parachute will open when you need it most. You don't shop for the cheapest parachute; you invest in the one that guarantees the outcome. The banker's higher price is the guarantee of the parachute opening—it's the certainty of execution.

Key Takeaways & The Banker's Toolkit

Key Takeaways

- **Anchor on Value First:** Never discuss the price until the client has fully agreed on the value proposition (the outcome, the certainty, the risk avoidance).

- **Refuse the Price War:** If a client mentions a competitor's lower price, reframe immediately: *"That is a cost comparison. Let's discuss the difference in risk exposure."*
- **The Cost of Failure:** Always translate your higher price into the Cost of Failure if they choose the cheaper option (e.g., "The 15% fee saving costs you 50 lakhs in penalty fees if the document is delayed").
- **Value is in the Invisible:** Focus on the non-seen, high-cost mitigation services: legal review, compliance assurance, and dedicated relationship manager availability.

Quick Action Plan: The 'Value Reframing Script'

1. **Acknowledge Price:** *"I understand Competitor X's price is lower."* (Validate their information).
2. **Pivot to Outcome:** *"However, the key is the outcome you require: guaranteed certainty. What is the financial cost if your shipment is delayed by one day?"*
3. **Justify the Delta:** "The difference in our price is exactly the cost of the insurance and certainty you are buying from us. That is the premium for the non-negotiable outcome."

Mental Tattoo

Price competes,
Value differentiates.

CHAPTER 22

Rich vs. Wealthy - The Foundational Concept for Sophisticated Advice

---

THE ANCHOR

"Richness is what you earn & Wealth is what earns for you".
— Author.

In the world of high-net-worth clients, the words Rich and Wealthy are often used interchangeably, but they represent a crucial strategic distinction. Rich is a high, quantifiable income stream—a high salary, a massive quarterly bonus, or a large, one-time sale of assets. It is transient and relies on active effort. Wealthy is a high, sustainable net worth—a perpetual cash flow generated by assets that require no active input. The strategic banker understands that the Rich client is focused on spending their income; the Wealthy client is focused on preserving and growing their asset base. Your goal is to advise the Rich client on how to transition their income into sustainable Wealth.

The Use Case Example: The Income Trap in Bengaluru

Meet Kavya, a Private Banker in Bengaluru, advising two clients who both earn ₹15 Crore per year:

1. **Client A (Rich):** Rakesh, a successful, high-profile corporate CEO. His ₹15 Crore income is based almost entirely on his salary and bonus, requiring 70-hour workweeks. His spending is high (large primary residence, leased luxury cars), and his net worth growth

is minimal. If Rakesh loses his job tomorrow, his income drops to zero. He is **Rich** but not yet Wealthy.

2. **Client B (Wealthy):** Meena, a successful retired entrepreneur. Her ₹15 Crore annual income is generated entirely by dividends from her private equity holdings and real estate rentals, which require no active management. Her net worth is high, and her spending is constrained by her asset returns. If Meena decides to stop working, her income remains stable. She is Wealthy.

- **The Strategic Failure:** A less differentiated advisory approach would treat both clients identically, anchoring recommendations on income size rather than income quality. This typically results in pitching high-risk, high-return products purely on the basis of earning capacity, overlooking the fundamentally different sustainability, risk exposure, and advisory needs of each client.
- **The Strategic Solution:** Kavya recognized the difference. For Rakesh (Rich), her advice focused on capital preservation, tax-efficient transfer of income into passive assets, and establishing an emergency liquidity pool—converting Richness into Wealth. For Meena (Wealthy), her advice focused on succession planning, portfolio diversification, and philanthropic trusts—protecting the established Wealth.

The failure point is treating high income as an indicator of lasting financial health. The strategic banker diagnoses the source and sustainability of the cash flow before advising.

The Strategic Distinction

Richness is high income that relies on active work; Wealth is high net worth that generates passive income.

Aspect	Rich (The Income Trap)	Wealthy (The Strategic Goal)
Source	**Active Income:** Salary, bonus, active business profit (Relies on the individual).	**Passive Income:** Dividends, interest, rents, asset appreciation (Relies on the portfolio).
Sustainability	**Transient:** Vulnerable to job loss, market downturns, or retirement.	**Sustainable:** Generates income while the individual sleeps.
Focus	**Consumption:** Focused on optimizing spending and maximizing lifestyle.	**Preservation:** Focused on optimizing tax structure and maximizing inter-generational transfer.
Banker's Role	To teach them how to **Convert Income** into Assets.	To teach them how to **Protect Assets** and structure their legacy.

The Strategic Analogy: The Financial Waterfall

Richness is a very large river that flows only because of constant rain (active effort). If the rain stops (loss of job/retirement), the river runs dry. Wealth is a deep, strategically managed reservoir: the input (active effort) is no longer needed because the structure itself generates the supply. The banker must help the client build the reservoir.

Key Takeaways & The Banker's Toolkit

Key Takeaways

- **The Banker's Mandate is to Create Wealth:** Your primary goal is to structure your client's finances to survive the loss of their active income.

- **Diagnose the Source:** Before pitching a product, ask: *"If you took a one-year sabbatical, how much of your current income would remain?"* The answer defines their true status.
- **Income is a Liability:** High active income often comes with high taxation and high spending obligations; advise clients to view it as the raw material for building passive assets.
- **Risk Tolerance:** The Rich client is often more risk-tolerant (because they believe they can earn it back); the Wealthy client is more risk-averse (because they prioritize preservation).

Quick Action Plan: The 'Sustainability Quotient'

1. **Calculate Passive Income:** Determine the client's current annual income generated *without* their active input (e.g., rentals + dividends).
2. **Calculate Core Expenses:** Determine the client's non-negotiable annual living expenses.
3. **The Quotient:** Advise that they are truly Wealthy only when their *Passive Income > Core Expenses.* Structure all advisory services around closing that gap.

Mental Tattoo

Richness shows on a statement,
Wealth shows on a balance sheet.

CHAPTER 23

Standardization vs. Tailoring (Personalisation & Customisation) - Escaping the Commodity Trap

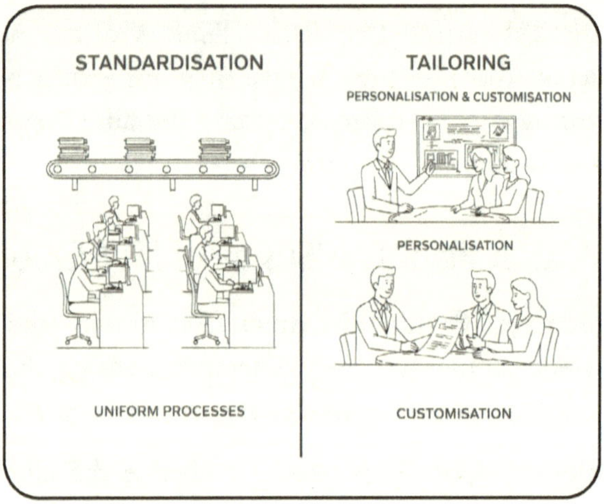

THE ANCHOR

The moment your solution fits everyone, it competes on price. Tailoring is how you escape that gravity — Author

---

In large financial institutions, the default operating model is Standardization—generic products, uniform pricing, and one-size-fits-all processes. Standardization optimizes for efficiency and scale, but it also strips the banker of differentiation. The strategic banker escapes this trap through Tailoring—the deliberate effort to adapt banking solutions to the client's real-life context. This tailoring takes two distinct forms:

Personalisation: Adapting communication, framing, and delivery so a standard product feels relevant.

Customisation: Altering the product structure itself to solve a client-specific problem.

The strategic skill is not choosing between them blindly, but knowing how much tailoring the situation truly requires.

The Use Case Example: The Mortgage That Looked Right—but Felt Wrong (Kolkata)

Meet Amrita, a Private Banker in Kolkata, advising Mr. and Mrs. Ghosh, a successful physician couple. Both doctors run independent practices with irregular quarterly cash flows, seasonal income spikes, and long-term plans to reduce clinical workload over the next decade. Their requirement was simple on the surface: *A home loan for a primary residence.* But beneath that simplicity lay a structural concern:

- Monthly EMIs conflicted with their uneven billing cycles
- Early repayment flexibility mattered more than headline interest rates
- Liquidity planning mattered more than speed of approval

The Standardization Trap:

Amrita's bank automatically issued a standardized mortgage offer:

- Fixed EMI schedule
- Generic interest rate
- Boilerplate communication

No reference to their profession or income pattern. The offer was *technically correct* but contextually blind. To the Ghosh's, it felt interchangeable—no different from any other large bank's proposal. The silent message was: *"This product works for everyone, so it should work for you."*

The Strategic Effort (The Solution):

Amrita recognized that the issue wasn't pricing—it was cash-flow alignment.

1. **Personalisation (Low Cost, High Impact):**

   She began with a conversation, not a product. She referenced how medical practices often experience quarterly income clustering and explained how specific features—like low prepayment penalties—could support accelerated debt reduction during surplus periods. The product stayed the same. *The meaning changed.*

2. **Customisation (High Cost, High Value):**

   As trust built, the Ghosh's asked a deeper question: *"Can the repayment structure reflect our quarterly income rather than monthly EMIs?"*

   Amrita escalated the request, redesigned the repayment structure, and secured special credit approval for a repayment holiday aligned to billing cycles. This bespoke structure converted relevance into commitment—and won the mandate.

The failure point is assuming standardization is sufficient for sophisticated clients. The strategic success lies in knowing when personalisation is enough—and when customisation becomes decisive.

The Strategic Distinction

Standardization is the default generic offer; Customisation & Personalisation is the strategic effort to tailor.

Aspect	Standardization (The Default Trap)	Tailoring (The Strategic Effort)
Effort Type	**Zero Effort:** Automated, one-size-fits-all, bulk communication.	**High Effort:** Either data-driven (Personalisation) or product-driven (Customisation).
Product Change	**None:** Delivering the exact same product to everyone.	**Customisation:** Product structure is fundamentally altered (e.g., bespoke contract). **Personalisation:** Product is unchanged, but the *delivery* is unique (e.g., unique language).
Cost to Bank	**Lowest:** Achieved through automation and scale.	**Highest:** Requires dedicated time, credit approval, and uniquc attention.
Client Perception	**Commodity:** You are interchangeable.	**Indispensable:** You are their unique, strategic partner.

The Strategic Analogy: The Financial Uniform

Standardization is forcing every client to wear the same financial uniform. Personalisation is ensuring that same uniform is delivered in the client's preferred color and size. Customisation is fundamentally redesigning the uniform to be a bespoke suit that fits only them. . The banker's job is to act as the tailor.

Key Takeaways & The Banker's Toolkit

Key Takeaways

- **Standardization is a ceiling, not a floor:** It is the fastest way to get replaced by a simple website.

- **Identify the Client's Threshold:** If the client is happy with Personalisation (data and context), do not waste effort on expensive Customisation.
- **Customisation is the Ultimate Barrier to Entry.** A competitor can copy your rate (Standardization) and your letter (Personalisation), but they cannot copy a uniquely structured, bespoke product.
- **Low-Cost Personalisation is Mandatory.** Use every piece of available client data (family, interests, business news) to enhance the delivery of every standardized interaction.

Quick Action Plan: The 'Tailoring Triage'

1. **Assess the Problem (Low/High):** Is the client's request manageable with a unique letter or phone call (Low Effort)? Or does it require a change to the core product/legal structure (High Effort)?
2. **Apply Personalisation First:** Always start by layering low-cost data and context onto the standard product.
3. **Deploy Customisation Strategically:** Only commit to the high-cost effort of Customisation when the deal size and long-term client value absolutely justify the non-scalable resource commitment.

Mental Tattoo

Standardized products are sold,
Tailored solutions are trusted.

CHAPTER 24

Customer Service vs. Customer Experience - The Strategic Difference Between Fixing Errors and Building Loyalty

---

THE ANCHOR

"The customer experience is the next competitive battleground."
— Jerry Gregoire

In banking, Customer Service is a crucial, reactive function: it's the immediate effort applied to address a request or fix a mistake *after* it has occurred. *Service is one necessary element within the overall client journey.* However, Customer Experience is the wholesome, proactive, and deliberate strategy and orchestration to manage the client's entire emotional and transactional journey. *Experience is the sum total of all various touchpoints*— from the initial welcome to the speed of the app and the follow-up email—and it must be designed for client delightment. The tomorrow's world of banking is all about Experience. The strategic banker understands that Service addresses a symptom; Experience addresses the system and builds a relationship moat.

The Use Case Example: The Delayed International Transfer in Pune

Meet Zoya, an SME Relationship Manager in Pune, whose client, Alpha Exports, frequently makes urgent international transfers to secure raw materials.

- **The Service Trap (Reactive Fix):** Alpha Exports initiates an urgent transfer of $500,000. It gets delayed for 48 hours due to an unforeseen compliance flag. The client calls Zoya, panicked. Zoya's team provides excellent Customer Service: they apologize profusely, resolve the issue, and waive the fee. The service element was perfect, but the client suffered 48 hours of anxiety, stress and operational risk. The incident created a negative memory, proving that *great service cannot fully compensate for a poor experience.*
- **The Experience Solution (Proactive Design):** A strategic Customer Experience approach would have anticipated the friction. Zoya's team, aware that such transactions often trigger compliance review, proactively called the client *before* the transfer was initiated, explaining:
  - The likely review window
  - The expected timeline
  - The escalation protocol

  During the four-hour compliance check, the team provided scheduled status updates every hour, even when there was no new information to share. Nothing went wrong — and nothing felt uncertain. The client experienced control, transparency, and reassurance. The transaction was no longer just successful; it was emotionally stable. The difference was not faster processing — it was designed communication validating the bank's strategic expertise and providing delightment through anticipation.

The failure point was allowing a predictable error to happen. The success of the Experience Solution was the wholesome design and responsive updates, managing the client's anxiety across all touchpoints.

The Strategic Distinction

Experience is the full journey designed for delightment; Service is the necessary repair component within that journey.

Aspect	Customer Service (The Reactive Component)	Customer Experience (The Strategic Asset)
Focus	**Failure Point:** Fixing errors and compensating for friction.	**All Touchpoints:** Proactively designing and executing every single client interaction.
Goal	**Resolution:** Getting the relationship back to neutral.	**Delightment & Loyalty:** Creating positive, memorable, and low-anxiety interactions across the whole cycle.
Scope	**Tactical:** An isolated interaction to fix a specific problem.	**Systemic & Wholesome:** The **sum total** of all operational, digital, and human interactions.
Tomorrow's Banking	**The Minimum Requirement:** Expected and easily copied.	**The Competitive Moat:** The decisive factor for client retention and future value.

The Strategic Analogy: The Financial Safety Net and the Ambulance

Customer Service is the ambulance that arrives quickly *after* a fall, treating the injury. It is a vital safety measure. Customer Experience is the proactive installation of a safety net and clear warning signs on the high wire, ensuring the client never falls in the first place, *and* providing clear communication during the crossing. The client values the safety net (proactive error avoidance) far more than the ambulance service.

Key Takeaways & The Banker's Toolkit

Key Takeaways

- **Experience is the sum of all parts:** Your website, your lobby, your app, your emails, and your team's tone are all critical touchpoints.
- **The Future is Design.** The tomorrow's banker designs the Experience (the system) before they rely on Service (the fix).
- **Experience is Anxiety Mitigation.** The goal is not just smooth transactions, but reducing the client's emotional uncertainty at every touchpoint (e.g., proactive updates).
- **Service is Costly.** Every hour spent fixing an error is an hour not spent on high-value client acquisition or strategic planning.

Quick Action Plan: The 'Friction Point Audit'

1. **Map the Client Journey:** Select one common client transaction (e.g., loan application) and map every single touchpoint, from the initial email to the final disbursement.
2. **Audit the Emotions:** At each touchpoint, ask: *"Does this moment reduce or increase client anxiety?"*
3. **Design the Delight:** For the three most anxious touchpoints, design a proactive intervention (update,

call, or automated prompt) to convert anxiety into delightment.

Mental Tattoo

Service resolves problems,
Experience reduces their frequency.

CHAPTER 25

Cross-Selling vs. Up-Selling - The Mastery of Wallet Share

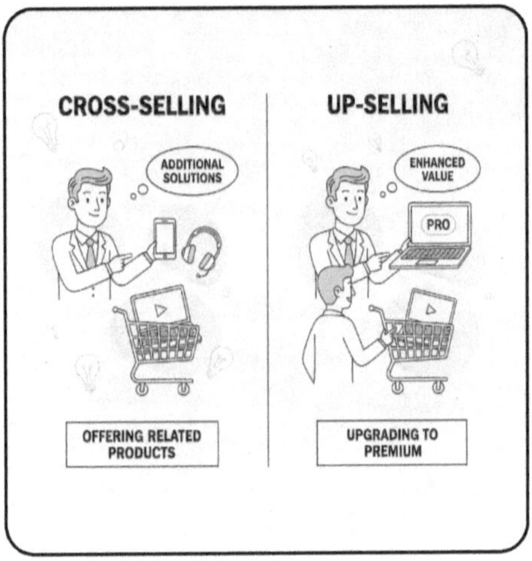

THE ANCHOR

"It is easier to sell to a client who already believes in you than to convince a new one." — Author

The growth of a financial institution is not driven by how many clients it acquires, but by how deeply it serves the clients it already has. In mature banking relationships, the real battlefield is not acquisition—it is wallet share. The tools for this are cross-selling and up-selling. While often confused as interchangeable growth tactics, they represent two fundamentally different strategic directions for deepening a relationship.

Up-selling optimizes a transaction on the other hand Cross-selling restructures a relationship. Mastery of this distinction determines whether you remain a single-product vendor or evolve into a multi-dimensional financial partner.

The Use Case Example: The Failed Wealth Manager in Kolkata

Meet Sumana, a motivated private wealth manager in Kolkata, managing the portfolio of Dr. Sanjay Sinha, a successful cardiologist. Dr. Sinha maintained a sizeable equity investment account with Sumana's bank and interacted with her regularly. Sumana's internal performance metric was clear: increase Average Assets Under Management (AUM) within her existing client book.

- **The Up-Selling Attempt:** Sumana focused her effort on a vertical upgrade. She pitched Dr. Sinha an upgrade from the standard equity account to the bank's Platinum Premium Account, highlighting:
  - Faster transaction processing
  - Priority service access
  - Status and exclusivity

However, the incremental value was marginal. From Dr. Sinha's perspective, the upgrade did not meaningfully change outcomes—only costs. He declined, stating that the current account already met his needs. The up-sell failed not because the product was weak, but because the value delta was insufficiently compelling.

- **The Missed Cross-Selling Opportunity:** What Sumana failed to diagnose was the *rest* of Dr. Sinha's financial ecosystem. In prior conversations, Dr. Sinha had casually mentioned:
    - Frequent international travel for medical conferences
    - Concerns about long-term protection for his dependents

These were not objections. They were signals. A strategic banker would have recognized at least two adjacent, unaddressed needs:

- *International Travel & FX Exposure* → International Travel Card / FX Solutions
- *Family Protection & Risk Management* → High-value Term Life Insurance

These were not upgrades to the same product. They were entirely new problem spaces. By ignoring these, Sumana focused narrowly on extracting incremental revenue from one product instead of expanding the bank's relevance across Dr. Sinha's financial life.

The result: No up-sell, No cross-sell & No increase in wallet share. The failure was not effort—it was direction.

The failure point was misdirecting effort. The critical insight is this

- *Up-selling is vertical* — more of the same product, justified only when the value leap is obvious.
- *Cross-selling is horizontal* — a new product solving a different risk, building dependency and loyalty.

Sumana focused on extracting a few more basis points from the existing relationship (Up-Sell failure) instead of solving an entirely new, unaddressed problem (Cross-Sell missed).

The Strategic Distinction

The difference between cross-selling and up-selling is defined by the axis of movement—Vertical vs. Horizontal—and the primary objective of the sale.

Aspect	Up-Selling (Vertical Growth)	Cross-Selling (Horizontal Growth)
Movement	**Depth:** Selling a superior, higher-priced version of the *same* product category.	**Breadth:** Selling a product from a **different** category or department.
Primary Goal	**Increased Revenue:** Maximizing the margin/size of the current transaction.	**Increased Stickiness:** Making the client dependent on more components of the bank.
Client Need Focus	**Better Quality/ Features** (e.g., higher credit limit, premium account).	**Unaddressed Need** (e.g., insurance, payment solutions, custody services).
Banker's Status	Product upgrade specialist.	**Full-service solution architect.**

The Strategic Analogy: The Financial Ecosystem

Think of the client's finances as an ecosystem. Up-selling is making a single tree bigger and taller (more revenue from one product). Cross-selling is planting a new, necessary type of tree—like adding a water filtration system (Trade Finance) or a fence (Insurance)—to complete the ecosystem. A truly sticky client is one who uses multiple bank components, making the cost of leaving prohibitively high. Cross-selling is the mastery of complexity that guarantees loyalty.

Key Takeaways & The Banker's Toolkit

Key Takeaways

- **Cross-selling creates loyalty; Up-selling creates immediate revenue:** Master both, but prioritize cross-selling for long-term retention.
- **The Diagnostic Question:** For up-selling, ask: "*How is the client limited by their current tier?*". For cross-selling, ask: "*Which major financial need are we* not *solving for them right now?*".
- **The Anchor Product:** Always ensure a successful cross-sell starts with a product that solves an immediate, tangible need, making it an *anchor* for future sales.
- The ideal time for an up-sell is often immediately after a successful, high-value cross-sell that has built immense trust.

Quick Action Plan: The 'Full Coverage Review'

1. **Map:** Use the client's current product (e.g., Equity Account) as the starting point, and verbally map the adjacent financial risk areas (insurance, succession, international payments).
2. **Ask Laterally:** Do not pitch the upgrade (Up-Sell) first. Ask a diagnostic question about the adjacent areas (Cross-Sell): "How are you currently handling your foreign currency exposure?"
3. **Prescribe:** Only introduce the necessary new product (e.g., International Travel Card) to fill that gap.

Mental Tattoo

**Up-Selling is getting a larger slice,
Cross-Selling is getting the whole pie.**

CHAPTER 26

Networking vs. Socializing - The Strategic Pursuit of Quality Connections

THE ANCHOR

"Your network is your net worth." — Porter Gale

In modern business, professionals mistake the sheer volume of contacts for strategic capital. Socializing (or 'Notworking') is the act of accumulating a large number of superficial contacts—attending many events, collecting business cards, and having surface-level conversations. It is low-effort and low-return. Networking is the strategic, high-effort pursuit of quality, high-trust connections built on mutual value and shared purpose. The strategic banker understands that one trusted, influential connection is worth a hundred casual contacts. The true measure of your network is not the size of your phone book, but the depth of trust and speed of reciprocity when you need assistance.

The Use Case Example: The Event Planner vs. The Connector in Bengaluru

Meet Rajiv, a Corporate Relationship Manager in Bengaluru who had recently been assigned coverage of private-equity-backed technology firms—a new segment for him. He was under pressure to originate his first meaningful mandate in this space and believed visibility was the fastest way to credibility.

The Socializing Trap (Notworking): Rajiv became relentlessly active. He attended multiple industry mixers, founder meetups, and investor conferences every month. His calendar was full, his evenings busy, and his LinkedIn connections steadily growing. At a high-profile CEO conference, Rajiv finally met the CFO of his target firm. They spoke for nearly twenty minutes—about the venue, the speakers, recent travel, and mutual acquaintances. The interaction was pleasant and polite. They exchanged contact details and connected online afterward.

Rajiv walked away feeling productive. Yet, because the conversation never moved beyond surface-level familiarity, it created no professional anchor. Within days, the CFO had no meaningful recollection of Rajiv or a reason to re-engage. Rajiv's effort produced activity—but no momentum.

The Networking Solution (Strategic Connection): Another banker, Sana, approached the same ecosystem differently. She attended far fewer events, but only those directly relevant to her target sector. At the same conference, Sana deliberately sought out the same CFO—not to introduce herself broadly, but to reference a specific regulatory tightening affecting PE-backed tech firms' cross-border cash structures. Rather than pitching a product, she offered perspective and context. She also mentioned that she could facilitate an introduction to a specialist regulatory advisor who had recently helped a similar firm navigate the issue. No mandate was discussed. No product was mentioned. But the interaction created immediate professional relevance. The CFO followed up within a week—not because Sana was memorable socially, but because she was useful strategically. That follow-up became the starting point of a relationship that later evolved into a mandate.

The failure point was Rajiv invested in visibility without relevance. Sana invested in relevance that created recall, trust, and reciprocity. Socializing maximized exposure. Networking maximized strategic memory.

The Strategic Distinction

Socializing is the accumulation of contacts; Networking is the strategic cultivation of high-value relationships.

Aspect	Socializing (The Volume Trap)	Networking (The Strategic Asset)
Focus	**Quantity:** Collecting cards, attending maximum events, maximizing reach.	**Quality:** Identifying key influencers, seeking common purpose, building mutual trust.
Motive	**Self-Interest:** Getting a lead, or avoiding looking busy (Social Pressure).	**Reciprocity:** Seeking ways to offer high, non-bank value first.
Engagement	**Shallow:** Superficial discussion, often focused on common pleasantries.	**Deep:** Inquiry into specific professional challenges and strategic goals.
Return	**Low:** Zero recall, few genuine referrals, high effort drain.	**High:** Trusted referrals, rapid access to decision-makers, high long-term ROI.

The Strategic Analogy: The Deal Funnel vs. The Trusted Shortcut

Socializing is building a very wide funnel—many conversations, many names, very little conversion. Networking is creating a trusted shortcut—fewer relationships, but faster access, deeper trust, and higher conversion probability. In banking, mandates rarely come from the widest funnel. They come from the shortest trusted path between problem and solution.

Key Takeaways & The Banker's Toolkit

Key Takeaways

- **Value over Volume:** Your time is capital; invest it only in connections where you can offer clear, specific value and where the trust is reciprocal.
- **The Reciprocity Test:** Never attend a networking event without a pre-planned answer to *"How can I help this person, even if they can't help me immediately?"*
- **Networking is not Selling.** Your goal is to build trust through non-transactional value, not pitch products at a social gathering.
- **The Connection Audit:** Review your last 20 contacts. If you cannot describe their three biggest professional challenges, you are Socializing, not Networking.

Quick Action Plan: The 'Strategic Connector'

1. **Define the Target:** Before attending any event, identify the *three most critical profiles* you need to meet (e.g., CFOs in the renewable energy sector).
2. **Define Your Value:** Prepare a specific, non-bank insight or introduction you can offer each profile (e.g., "I know a specialized tax consultant for solar projects").
3. **The Follow-Up Filter:** After the meeting, categorize the contact*: A (High Trust/Reciprocity), B (Future Potential), C (Socializing/Delete).* Ruthlessly focus your time only on A and B contacts.

Mental Tattoo

Socializing collects contacts,
Networking cultivates connectors.

CHAPTER 27

Loyalty vs. Satisfaction - The Strategic Difference Between Happiness and Commitment

---

THE ANCHOR

"Loyalty is when people are willing to pay a premium and advocate for you". — Shep Hyken

---

In banking, Satisfaction is the minimum requirement for survival; Loyalty is the strategic asset that guarantees long-term profit. Satisfaction is a transactional feeling—the client is currently happy with the fees, the speed of service, or the market returns. It is fragile, temporary, and easily bought by a competitor offering a 10 basis-point advantage. Loyalty is a deep, emotional commitment—the client is bound by a sense of shared purpose, trust (as defined in Chapter 14), and personal connection. *The strategic banker understands that Satisfaction is easily earned and instantly lost; Loyalty is painstakingly built but endures market volatility.*

The Use Case Example: The Satisfied but Switched Client in Pune

Meet Kishore, a Branch Manager in Pune, who managed the relationship of Ms. Priya Reddy, a successful restaurateur operating multiple premium outlets across the city. Over several years, Ms. Reddy consolidated her working capital lines, merchant payments, and personal investments with Kishore's branch.

- **The Satisfaction Trap (Transient Happiness):** Ms. Reddy was highly Satisfied. She regularly praised Kishore's efficiency. She appreciated the branch's professional ambience, the familiarity of the staff, the predictable turnaround time, and the competitive pricing on her loans. Her interactions were smooth, efficient, and frictionless. Kishore interpreted this happiness as secure Loyalty and this comfort as stability. He focused on maintaining operational excellence—rates, service levels, and responsiveness—believing that satisfaction naturally translated into loyalty. What he missed was depth. Conversations rarely moved beyond transactions. There were no strategic discussions about expansion risk, succession planning, or stress scenarios in her business. The relationship was pleasant—but shallow.
- **The Loyalty Failure (The Rational Exit):** Three years into the relationship, a new, aggressively priced digital bank offered Ms. Reddy a corporate line of credit that was 50 basis points cheaper and offered a slightly better app experience with dashboard tailored for multi-location businesses. The offer was objectively attractive—but not extraordinary. Ms. Reddy switched. Because Ms. Reddy's relationship with Kishore was based only on current transactional Satisfaction (price, service), the decision to switch was purely rational and easy. There was no emotional or personal cost attached to leaving. There was no hesitation, no internal conflict, and no sense of loss. Kishore lost a high-value client because his effort built happiness, not commitment. It delivered satisfaction, not attachment.

The failure point was that Kishore confused the client's transient happiness with deep commitment. The competitor bought the relationship for a negligible price because Kishore failed to build a "moat of loyalty." Satisfaction delayed the exit. Loyalty would have prevented it.

The Strategic Distinction

Satisfaction is easily purchased and easily lost; Loyalty is emotionally earned and highly resilient.

Aspect	Satisfaction (The Transient Feeling)	Loyalty (The Strategic Commitment)
Foundation	**Transaction:** Current price, product quality, speed, and fee structure.	**Emotion:** Personal trust, shared values, and perceived indispensable partnership.
Decision Driver	**Rational/Price:** Does the competitor offer a better quantifiable deal?	**Emotional/Value:** Is the pain of leaving greater than the small financial gain?
Duration	**Short-Term:** Lasts only until a better offer arrives.	**Long-Term:** Endures market downturns and competitive price challenges.
Banker's Goal	To be **Good** (Meeting current needs).	To be **Irreplaceable** (Creating commitment).

The Strategic Analogy: The Subscription vs. The Membership

Satisfaction is a subscription. The client stays as long as the service is good and the price feels fair. Cancelling is easy. Loyalty is a membership. It carries identity, trust, and emotional investment. Leaving feels disruptive—even if alternatives exist.

In banking, competitors can always offer a better subscription. Only you can build a membership.

Key Takeaways & The Banker's Toolkit

Key Takeaways

- **Loyalty is Your Moat:** Your goal is to make the act of leaving your bank feel emotionally and strategically painful for the client.
- **The 10-Basis-Point Test:** If the client would leave you for a 10-basis-point better deal from a competitor, you have a Satisfaction relationship, not a Loyalty relationship.
- **Loyalty is Non-Monetized:** The effort that generates true loyalty involves non-revenue-generating actions: calling during a crisis, offering personal introductions, or giving strategic advice outside your product mandate.
- **Measure Commitment, Not Happiness:** Use strategic questions to gauge true loyalty (e.g., "If you could switch tomorrow for a 1% gain, would you?").

Quick Action Plan: The 'Commitment Builder'

1. **Map the Personal Connection:** Identify three key, non-financial data points about the client (e.g., child's college, favored charity, golf interest). Use one of these in the next interaction.
2. **The Pro Bono Moment:** Once per quarter, provide the client with a high-value insight or connection (e.g., a lawyer referral, a specific industry report) that generates zero fee for the bank. This signals commitment over transaction.

3. **Cross-Functional Hook:** Ensure the client has deep relationships with at least three different people or divisions within your bank (e.g., Wealth, Corporate, and Treasury). This makes the logistical barrier to leaving extremely high (creating a "switching cost").

Mental Tattoo

Satisfaction ends with delivery,
Loyalty begins after it.

CHAPTER 28

Persuasion vs. Manipulation - The Ethical Line Between Influence and Exploitation

---

THE ANCHOR

"Integrity is not a strategy choice, it is the operating system".
— Author

In the strategic world of finance, every deal requires influence. Persuasion is the ethical application of influence: using logic, data, and value-based arguments to lead the client to a decision that is mutually beneficial and strategically sound for them. Manipulation is the unethical abuse of influence: exploiting the client's emotions, urgency, or lack of knowledge for the bank's singular gain. The strategic banker understands that Persuasion builds long-term trust and loyalty; Manipulation earns a quick fee but instantly destroys a career and a reputation. The ethical line between the two is defined by transparency and intent.

The Use Case Example: The Commission-Driven Recommendation in Hyderabad

Meet Veer, a Relationship Manager in Hyderabad, pitching investment products to Mr. Srinivas, a high-net-worth individual who had recently received a large liquidity event. Veer knew Mr. Srinivas was risk-averse.

- **The Manipulation Trap:** Veer was under internal pressure to close the sale of the bank's proprietary, high-commission Structured Product (SP) before his quarter end review. Veer knew the SP was complex, carried a high exit penalty, and was slightly too aggressive for Mr. Srinivas's conservative profile. Veer failed to clearly explain the exit penalty, highlighted only the best-case historical returns, and used emotional pressure by stating the "window was closing tomorrow." This was Manipulation—driving the client to a detrimental decision purely for Veer's commission.

- **The Persuasion Solution:** A truly persuasive banker, even needing the fee, would have anchored the conversation to the client's defined risk profile. They would have used transparency, stating clearly: *"Based on your risk profile, this Structured Product (SP) is slightly aggressive. I recommend a lower-fee, guaranteed fixed deposit strategy. However, the SP offers higher potential returns, paired with a clearly defined exit penalty and limited liquidity if you need to unwind the position early. I advise against it, but if you wish to allocate a small portion, you must understand the risk."* By slowing the decision instead of accelerating it, the banker demonstrated confidence in the advice rather than urgency in the sale. By being transparent about the risks and the exit penalties, the banker maintained Persuasion—focusing on the client's interests—rather than exploiting their ignorance (Manipulation).

The failure point was that Veer prioritized a one-time commission over the client's long-term financial health. Manipulation won the short-term sale but guaranteed the eventual loss of the entire relationship.

The Strategic Distinction

Persuasion uses transparency and value for mutual gain; Manipulation uses deceit and pressure for selfish gain.

Aspect	Manipulation (The Unethical Trap)	Persuasion (The ethical Advantage)
Foundation	**Deception/Omission:** Withholding negative facts (e.g., hidden fees, exit penalties).	**Transparency/Logic:** Full disclosure of risk and reliance on data and value.
Motive	**Self-Interest:** Achieving the banker's personal target or bonus.	**Mutual Benefit:** Achieving the client's goal while earning a fair fee.
Technique	**Emotional Pressure:** Using urgency, fear, or guilt (e.g., "The window is closing").	**Value-Based Argument:** Linking the solution to the client's previously defined need.
Long-Term Impact	**Reputation Destruction:** Creates client distrust and regulatory risk.	**Relationship Building:** Fosters deep trust and guarantees referrals.

The Strategic Analogy: The Financial Map

Manipulation is giving the client a map that strategically omits the dangerous swamps and cliffs, leading them to a destination that only benefits you. Persuasion is giving the client a full, accurate map, clearly marking all the risks and pitfalls, and then advising them on the best, safest route to their desired destination. . The client must trust the map and the navigator.

Key Takeaways & The Banker's Toolkit

Key Takeaways

- **Trust is not negotiable:** One manipulative act can destroy years of relationship-building.
- **The Exit Penalty Rule:** Always disclose the three most painful or negative aspects of the product (the exit

penalty, the worst-case scenario, the maximum fee) before discussing the upside.

- **Use Data, Not Emotion:** Persuasion relies on facts and analysis; manipulation relies on emotional urgency. Never use *"You must decide now."*
- **The Integrity Test:** Ask yourself: *"If the client was my own parent, would I still recommend this product in this exact manner?"*

Quick Action Plan: The 'Transparency Checklist'

1. **Map the Risk:** List the three worst things that could happen to the client if the product fails or the market moves against them.
2. **Verbalize the Negative:** Start the final pitch section by reading the three mapped risks aloud to the client. This builds ethical credibility and disarms the need for emotional pressure.
3. **Offer the Out:** Conclude the conversation with a statement that removes urgency: "This is a significant decision. Please take 48 hours to discuss it with your partner or advisor."

Mental Tattoo

Persuasion seeks shared benefit,
Manipulation seeks selfish gain.

PART IV:
The Legacy - Ownership, Ethics, and Growth

The Final Ascent

If success in the previous parts was measured in closed deals and professional credibility, success in *Part IV* is measured in *enduring character and reputation.* This section distils the non-negotiable personal principles that underpin a long-term, ethical, and elite career in finance. This is where the successful banker separates themselves from the fleeting success of the transactional salesperson.

This is the final separation.

- *Part I* taught you how to *think.*
- *Part II* taught you how to *engage and speak*
- *Part III* taught you how to *win.*
- *Part IV teaches you how to endure , lead and how to be trusted with power.*

These final distinctions address the foundational pillars of elite performance: the mastery of time, the commitment to ethical rigor, and the relentless pursuit of perfection in execution.

Your Progression Through Part IV

This part is deliberately structured as a progression from personal integrity to organizational impact, and finally to enduring legacy:

1. **Ethical Bedrock (Integrity, Principle, Risk)**: You begin with the non-negotiables: choosing integrity over compliance, principle over policy, and calculated risk-taking over reckless behaviour. These chapters define how leaders act when rules are insufficient and consequences are real.

2. **Ownership & Authority (Accountability, Trust, Delegation)** : You then move into true ownership: the

difference between *responsibility and accountability, authority and trust, and delegation versus dumping*. This is where managers stop supervising work—and leaders start owning outcomes through others.

3. **People & Growth (Mentorship, Economics, Mindshare, Teams)** : Leadership scales through people and judgment. These chapters clarify the difference between *mentors and sponsors, revenue and margin, market share and mindshare, and talent versus teams*. This is the shift from individual performance to institutional strength.
4. **Enduring Impact (Leadership & Legacy)**: You conclude with the final transition: *management versus leadership, and success versus legacy*. These chapters ask the ultimate question: *When you step away, what still works because you were here?*

Part IV is not about being impressive. It is about being *reliable under pressure, ethical under temptation, and trusted with scale*. Mastering these distinctions is how professionals stop chasing advancement—and *start earning permanence*. This is not the loudest part of the book. It is the part that lasts the longest.

No	Core Distinction	The Strategic Progression
29.	Integrity vs. Compliance	The foundational ethical choice: upholding principle versus following the minimum rule.
30.	Policy vs. Principle	Applying ethics and values when the rulebook is silent or ambiguous.
31.	Risk-Taking vs. Recklessness	Strategic decision-making: calculated moves versus gambling on outcomes.

No	Core Distinction	The Strategic Progression
32.	Accountability vs. Responsibility	The ultimate ownership: taking charge of the final result, not just the task.
33.	Trust vs. Authority	Earning command versus demanding obedience from your team.
34.	Delegation vs. Dumping	Empowering teams correctly or simply abandoning tasks.
35.	Mentor vs. Sponsor	Guidance or active promotion of talent.
36.	Revenue vs. Margin	Chasing topline growth versus building sustainable profitability through disciplined pricing, cost awareness, and client selection.
37.	Market share vs. Mindshare	Being widely present versus being deeply remembered and instinctively trusted when critical decisions are made.
38.	Talent vs. Team	Relying on individual brilliance versus deliberately building a coordinated, complementary system that outperforms any single star.
39.	Management vs. Leadership	The core transition: directing tasks or inspiring people.
40.	Success vs. Legacy	Personal achievement within a tenure or building systems, people, and standards that outlast the individual.

CHAPTER 29

Integrity vs. Compliance - The Ethical Line Between Following Rules and Upholding Principles

THE ANCHOR

"Integrity shows up when rules run out". — Author

In the financial industry, Compliance is the enforced regulatory baseline. It is an external obligation—adhering to prescribed laws, regulatory circulars, internal policies, audit trails, and checklists designed to protect the institution from legal and supervisory action. Compliance answers the question: "Have we met the minimum requirement?"

Integrity, however, is the self-imposed internal standard. It governs behavior in gray zones where rules are silent, ambiguous, or technically satisfied but ethically incomplete. Integrity answers a more difficult question: *"Is this transaction fundamentally right, transparent, and defensible over time?"*

The strategic banker understands that Compliance protects the bank from regulators; Integrity protects the bank's reputation, the client's credibility, and the banker's career longevity. The difference between the two is the gap between passing an audit and earning trust that compounds over decades.

The Use Case Example: The Ambiguous Trust Documents in Mumbai

Meet Aisha, a Private Banker in Mumbai, onboarding a highly profitable, new client who is transferring assets through a complex Family Trust. The deal is critical for Aisha to hit her quarter-end targets.

- **The Compliance Trap (Minimum Standard):** The client submitted documentation that technically satisfied the bank's KYC checklist—trust deed, settlor details, trustee identification, and current asset statements. From a checklist perspective, the onboarding could proceed. However, Aisha noticed a gap: the Source of Initial Wealth that originally funded the trust—specifically, documentation linking the seed capital to historical business exits and legacy asset sales—was summarized but not independently validated through sale agreements, tax filings, or legacy bank statements.

  The Compliance team, under workload pressure, would likely approve the file as "technically complete." Proceeding would have met the letter of the law, but left a blind spot in understanding long-term reputational and regulatory exposure.

- **The Integrity Solution (Highest Standard):** Instead of delaying silently or escalating defensively, Aisha acted with precision. She went back to the client and explained: "*To future-proof this relationship—for you and for us—we need documented clarity on how the trust was originally capitalized. This protects you from future scrutiny and ensures your structure remains unquestioned under any regulatory review.*" She requested specific, targeted documents:
    - Historical sale agreements of the originating businesses
    - Corresponding tax filings evidencing declared proceeds
    - One legacy bank statement linking proceeds to the trust funding

Crucially, Aisha did not allow ethics to become an excuse for inefficiency. She coordinated internally—pre-briefing Compliance, Risk, and Operations—so that once the final documents arrived, the account was approved and activated without delay, meeting the client's urgency while raising the ethical bar. The client appreciated that the banker was protecting not just the bank, but their own reputation and future scrutiny risk. Integrity did not slow the deal—it strengthened it.

The failure point is allowing the external pressure of targets to override the internal principle of strategic risk clarity. Compliance is transactional; Integrity is foundational.

The Strategic Distinction

Integrity is the internal principle; Compliance is the external rule.

Aspect	Compliance (The External Minimum)	Integrity (The Internal Principle)
Driver	**Fear/Punishment:** Avoiding fines, regulatory action, or disciplinary measures.	**Values/Principle:** Doing the right thing because it is morally and strategically correct.
Standard	**The Letter of the Law:** What the rule *requires* you to do.	**The Spirit of the Law:** What the rule *intends* you to achieve (full transparency, zero risk).
Scope	**Reactive:** Checklists and controls to manage existing rules.	**Proactive:** Anticipating future regulatory changes or ethical gray areas.
Impact	**Protects the Bank's Wallet** (from fines).	**Protects the Bank's Reputation** (the most valuable asset).

The Strategic Analogy: The Financial Firewall

Compliance is like having a perfectly functional, up-to-date regulatory firewall that stops known external threats (known viruses). Integrity is the internal culture that ensures no employee ever introduces a thumb drive containing a risk to the system, even when the firewall cannot see it. The strategic banker operates at the level of Integrity because the firewall (Compliance) cannot protect against internal ethical compromise.

Key Takeaways & The Banker's Toolkit

Key Takeaways

- **Compliance is easily outsourced; Integrity is non-negotiable character:** You cannot delegate your ethical standard.

- **The Reputation Test:** Before pushing a deal, ask: *"If this transaction were published on the front page of the financial newspaper tomorrow, would I be proud of the ethical scrutiny?"*
- **Integrity is Long-Term Risk Management.** Choosing the higher ethical standard is the lowest-cost way to manage future litigation and reputational damage.
- **Never Hide Behind the Checklist.** If the transaction *feels* wrong, the minimum compliance checklist is irrelevant. The feeling is your warning sign.

Quick Action Plan: The 'Grey Area Audit'

1. **Identify the Loophole:** Whenever a deal is structured using a loophole or a technicality that avoids the *intent* of a rule, flag it as a Compliance risk.
2. **Ask the 'Why':** Ask the client: "Why are we doing it this way instead of the standard, most transparent way?" The answer reveals their intent and the ethical risk.
3. **Offer the Ethical Upgrade:** Proactively recommend the path of highest Integrity, even if it adds friction or cost. Frame it as necessary for long-term strategic partnership (e.g., "This extra step ensures zero questions from any future audit").

Mental Tattoo

Compliance keeps you legal,
Integrity keeps you credible.

CHAPTER 30

Policy vs. Principle - The Strategic Difference Between Following the Guidebook and Upholding the Mandate

---

THE ANCHOR

"Principles are eternal truths; policies are temporary rules."
— Author

In banking, Policy is the codified, written rule for specific, repeatable situations—credit caps, exposure limits, approval hierarchies, collateral requirements, sectoral limits, pricing floors, delegation matrices, and documentation checklists (for example, lending caps linked to 25% of net worth or mandatory collateral thresholds). Policies are designed to standardize judgment, reduce variance, and protect the institution when decisions are made at scale. They are necessary guardrails—but by design, they assume averages, not exceptional client contexts. Principle, however, is the fundamental, non-negotiable guiding truth that underpins every sound banking decision. It reflects the bank's core beliefs about risk, sustainability, and stewardship—such as lending only where cash flows are durable and transparent, preserving capital across cycles, minimizing contingent liabilities, and protecting the institution's reputation above short-term gains. Principles do not change with circulars or credit cycles; they exist to guide judgment when policies fall silent, conflict, or fail to capture the reality of an exceptional case. The strategic banker understands that Policy guides the amateur; Principle empowers the leader to make strategic exceptions that drive profitable growth. When a Policy restricts a great client, the leader must appeal to the higher Principle.

The Use Case Example: The Guarantee Cap Exception in Bengaluru

Meet Divya, a Corporate Relationship Manager in Bengaluru, who is managing a major, multi-year client, TechWiz Manufacturing. TechWiz is highly profitable but currently has low reported net worth due to recent, accelerated debt repayment. They urgently require a non-fund-based facility (a guarantee) for a critical new contract.

- **The Policy Trap (Rigid Rule):** The bank's credit manual strictly states that all non-fund-based guarantees for manufacturing clients must be capped at 25% of the client's current net worth. TechWiz needs a guarantee for 35% of its net worth. The rigid banker would simply say, "The Policy doesn't allow it, I can only offer 25%," sacrificing the strategic client and the fee. This ends the dialogue and the potential growth.
- **The Principle Solution (Strategic Appeal):** Divya understands that the true Principle behind the 25% guarantee cap is not the number itself, but the protection of the bank against *uncontrolled contingent liability during stress scenarios* like during business downturn. She goes deeper than the balance sheet.

  She analyzes TechWiz's underlying risk drivers:

  - The guarantee is backed by confirmed, milestone-based government contracts

- Cash flows from these contracts are ring-fenced and escrowed
- The contract tenor is shorter than the guarantee tenure assumed by policy
- Historical execution risk is negligible

Instead of asking for a "policy exception," Divya reframes the request to the Credit Committee:

"The policy assumes contingent risk based on net worth alone. In this case, the real risk is governed by contract certainty and cash-flow visibility, both of which materially exceed policy assumptions. Approving this facility does not weaken the policy—it fulfills its intent." By anchoring the discussion on risk substance rather than policy form, Divya secures approval, protects the bank, and establishes herself as a banker who understands *why* rules exist—not just *what* they say.

The failure point is rigidly applying the *letter* of the Policy without understanding the underlying *Principle.* Policy is a guideline for risk mitigation; Principle is the truth for strategic growth.

The Strategic Distinction

Policy is the situation guide; Principle is the fundamental truth.

Aspect	Policy (The Codified Rule)	Principle (The Guiding Truth)
Source	**External/Written:** Found in the bank's manual and subject to regular revision.	**Internal/Foundational:** Derived from core business philosophy and ethical mandate.

Aspect	Policy (The Codified Rule)	Principle (The Guiding Truth)
Flexibility	**Low:** Designed for mass application and appeals require formal exception.	**High:** Used by leaders to interpret gray areas and define strategic exceptions.
Language	**"What to Do":** Operational instruction for specific figures (e.g., "Cap at 25%").	**"Why to Do It":** The strategic mandate (e.g., "Minimize contingent risk").
Function	To manage **Risk** across the general portfolio.	To enable **Strategic Growth** in specific, justified instances.

The Strategic Analogy: The Financial GPS

Policy is the turn-by-turn instruction given by the GPS: rigid, numerical, and easy to follow. If there's a road closure, the rigid driver stops. Principle is the knowledge of the overall city map and the destination. The strategic banker, when the Policy (GPS) fails, uses the Principle (the map) to find a better, quicker, and safer route to the goal. Policies change; Principles endure.

Key Takeaways & The Banker's Toolkit

Key Takeaways

- **Policy is for the masses; Principle is for the elite:** Do not let a guideline obstruct a clearly justifiable strategic outcome.
- **Challenge the 'Why':** When a Policy limits a profitable deal, ask: "What strategic Principle is this Policy designed to protect?" If the deal does not violate the Principle, appeal the Policy.

- **Never Appeal Policy for Convenience.** Appeal to Principle only when the exception is objectively cleaner and lower-risk than the scenario the Policy was designed to prevent.
- **Policy is Your Backup.** In moments of uncertainty, the Policy protects you. In moments of strategic clarity, the Principle empowers you.

Quick Action Plan: The 'Principle Appeal'

1. **Identify the Policy Barrier:** Note the specific rule or number stopping the deal (e.g., "25% Cap").
2. **Define the Governing Principle:** Clearly articulate the core risk that the Policy aims to mitigate (e.g., "Contingent Liability Minimization").
3. **Construct the Argument:** Prove that the client's unique circumstances uphold the Principle even while breaking the Policy (e.g., "The government-backed contract reduces the contingent risk to 5%, far below the Policy's assumed risk level").

> **Mental Tattoo**
>
> **Policy governs behavior and action,**
> **Principle governs judgement and decision.**

CHAPTER 31

Risk-Taking vs. Recklessness - The Strategic Difference Between Calculated Courage and Blind Impatience

THE ANCHOR

"Risk comes from not knowing what you are doing." — Warren Buffett

In finance, taking Risk is mandatory for generating superior returns. However, the line between Risk-Taking and Recklessness is the most dangerous line a banker will ever cross. Recklessness is the act of taking high-risk action without due diligence, a stress-tested exit plan, or an asymmetric payoff (where the downside outweighs the upside). It is emotional and driven by impatience or greed. Risk-Taking, conversely, is a disciplined action: meticulous analysis of the downside, hedging strategies, and a clear understanding that the potential reward is strategically justified. The strategic banker never avoids risk; they manage it, mitigate it, and monetize it.

The Use Case Example: The M&A Bridge Financing in Mumbai

Meet Kabir, an Investment Banker in Mumbai, who is advising a high-growth tech client, NovaSoft, on a massive, time-sensitive acquisition. NovaSoft needs a ₹500 Crore bridge loan to close the deal within 72 hours while waiting for a larger institutional funding round (the takeout) to finalize.

- **The Recklessness Trap (Blind Impatience):** Kabir's junior team, eager for the massive fee, pushes the loan through the committee with minimal due diligence. They accept the client's aggressive valuation of the target company without verifying its intellectual property (IP) assets and ignore a recent, unresolved litigation issue. They prioritized the fee and the deadline over the analytical validation of the risk. This is Reckless—it guarantees the bank will fully absorb the cost if the deal sours or the takeout fails.
- **The Risk-Taking Solution (Calculated Courage):** The strategic banker, Kabir, recognizes the high fee but demands a full-day diagnostic sprint on the target company's accounts and legal history. He identifies the core risks: the litigation and the lack of a guaranteed takeout buyer. Kabir agrees to take the Risk, but only after structuring the deal to protect the bank:

    1. He reduces the loan principal by 10% (mitigating the downside).
    2. He includes a specific, legally binding break clause tied to the resolution of the identified litigation (creating an exit).
    3. He requires a high-certainty commitment from the takeout buyers (ensuring repayment).

Kabir successfully took a high Risk, but because he managed and mitigated the downside analytically, the decision was strategically sound. Recklessness is gambling; Risk-Taking is calculated investment.

The failure point occurs when urgency replaces analysis. The moment Kabir's team allowed the deadline and fee to override due diligence, the decision stopped being strategic and became emotional. By accepting the client's assumptions without verification, they silently transferred all downside risk to the bank while preserving none of the optionality. This is where most bankers fail: they confuse speed with decisiveness and conviction with courage. True risk-taking pauses to protect the downside, recklessness rushes forward hoping the upside will save the decision.

The Strategic Distinction

Risk-Taking is analytical and protects the downside; Recklessness is emotional and ignores the analysis.

Aspect	Recklessness (The Emotional Reaction)	Risk-Taking (The Strategic Discipline)
Analysis	**Minimal/Ignored:** Driven by opportunity, greed, or deadline pressure.	**Meticulous:** Full stress-testing of the downside scenario (worst-case).
Mitigation	**None:** Focusing only on the upside potential.	**Mandatory:** Structuring the deal with clear hedges, guarantees, or break clauses.
Outcome Asymmetry	**Poor:** Downside (loss) is larger than or equal to the potential upside.	**Favorable:** Upside (reward) is far greater than the maximum, mitigated loss.
Ethos	**Gambling:** Prioritizing excitement over intelligence.	**Investing:** Prioritizing long-term profitability and preservation of capital.

The Strategic Analogy: The Financial Safety Ratio

Recklessness is driving an F1 car at 300 km/h with bald tires and no brake pads—hoping you win the race without a crash. Risk-Taking is driving an F1 car at 300 km/h only after the engineers have verified the tires, brakes, and safety harness, knowing that the potential reward justifies the highly controlled speed. . The strategic banker focuses on the safety ratio first.

Key Takeaways & The Banker's Toolkit

Key Takeaways

- **Never Go All-In Blindly:** Strategic risk requires conviction, but conviction must be supported by analytical rigor.
- **The Worst-Case Scenario:** Before you approve a high-risk deal, you must be able to articulate exactly how much the bank stands to lose and when that loss would occur.
- **Mitigation Over Avoidance:** The best bankers don't say "No" to risk; they say, "Yes, provided we secure X, Y, and Z protection."
- **The Asymmetry Principle:** A true strategic risk requires that the potential gain be at least 3x greater than the maximum potential loss.

Quick Action Plan: The 'Downside Protection Checklist'

1. **Map the Failure:** Identify the single event that would cause the deal to fail (e.g., Target company litigation is lost).
2. **Define the Break Clause:** Build a legal clause into the contract that allows the bank to exit or adjust the terms immediately if the failure event occurs.
3. **Hedge the Exposure:** Require the client to provide guaranteed, verifiable collateral that covers at least 150% of the loan amount *specifically* in the event of failure.

Mental Tattoo

Recklessness is reacting,
Risk-Taking is calculating.

CHAPTER 32

Accountability vs. Responsibility: The Difference Between Doing the Task and Owning the Outcome

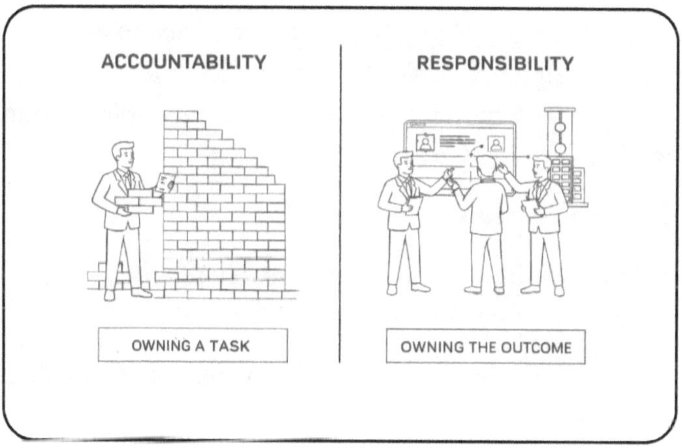

THE ANCHOR

"Accountability is the willingness to answer for the outcomes, not the activity." —Author

In a large financial institution, responsibility is easy to distribute. Tasks are assigned, roles are defined, and ownership is segmented across teams, systems, and hierarchies. Processing a trade, submitting a document, approving a checklist—these are all responsibilities. But true professionalism, and true leadership, is defined by accountability. Accountability is rare and not assigned. Responsibility is delegated; accountability is voluntarily owned. When a financial process fails, the person who was responsible did the job, but the person who is accountable accepts the failure and fixes the systemic cause. Responsibility answers *"Was my task done?"* Accountability answers *"Did the client get the outcome?"* Mastering this distinction is crucial for navigating hierarchies and advancing a career.

The Use Case Example: The Missing Compliance Document in Hyderabad

Meet Abhishek, a Bank Operations Manager based in Noida, responsible for overseeing trade finance documentation for multiple corporate clients. One of his key clients is Avantika Iron Corp, an exporter executing a time-critical shipment backed by a Letter of Credit (LC).

The Problem Statement

- Avantika Iron Corp submitted all required compliance documents on time.
- The bank has an internal cut-off of 4:00 PM for uploading and validating documents so the LC can be processed the same day.
- Due to an internal queue-monitoring lapse, the documents were not uploaded into the system before cut-off, causing a one-day delay in LC issuance.
- This delay risked shipment disruption and damaged client confidence.

The failure was internal to the bank, not client-driven. The issue was escalated to the Head of Trade Finance (bank side), who asked Abhishek for an explanation.

- **The Responsibility Trap (Task Ownership)**

  Abhishek responded: "*The documents were submitted by the client on time. However, my junior associate Ramesh was responsible for monitoring the upload queue at 4 PM, and he missed this item. It was his responsibility."*

What this response does:

- Correctly identifies task ownership
- Shifts blame downward
- Treats the incident as an individual lapse, not a process failure
- Does nothing to repair client trust or prevent recurrence

  From a hierarchy perspective, Abhishek protected himself. From a leadership perspective, he failed.

- **The Accountability Solution (Outcome Ownership)**

  An accountable response would have been: "*The client submitted the documents on time, but the bank missed the cut-off. I am accountable for this outcome. I am personally calling Avantika Iron Corp to manage the impact today, and I am implementing a mandatory dual-check escalation for all LC uploads near cut-off so this cannot happen again.*"

What this response does:

- Clearly accepts bank-side ownership
- Separates root cause analysis from client communication
- Fixes the system, not just the symptom
- Preserves the client relationship while maintaining internal discipline

Internally, Ramesh can still be coached. Externally, the bank speaks with one accountable voice.

The failure point was transferring ownership. In the client's eyes, Abhishek, the bank's face, was accountable for the outcome. Abhishek's focus on Ramesh's responsibility damaged both his credibility with management and his team's morale, while doing nothing to repair the client relationship.

The Strategic Distinction

Responsibility is the assigned task; accountability is the moral and professional ownership of the result.

Aspect	Responsibility (The Assigned Task)	Accountability (The Owned Outcome)
Focus	**Task Completion** ("Did I do my part?").	**Final Result** ("Did the client get the outcome?").
Motive	Driven by **compliance** (checking the box).	Driven by **integrity** (owning the consequence).
Client Perception	**Bureaucratic** ("They follow rules").	**Reliable** ("They make things right").
Consequence	Can be **delegated** or shared with a team.	Must be **personally owned** by the leader/ banker.

The Strategic Analogy: The Financial Supply Chain

In banking, your service is a complex financial supply chain. In banking, dozens of hands touch a single transaction—credit, legal, ops, compliance. Responsibility lives at each touchpoint. Every employee is responsible for their step (e.g., credit analysis, legal sign-off, trade processing). Accountability lives at the deal level. The accountable banker is the one who steps outside the chain, views the process from the client's perspective, and guarantees that the client receives the final, satisfactory product, regardless of which individual step failed. Accountability is seeing the entire trade deal, not just your document desk.

Key Takeaways & The Banker's Toolkit

Key Takeaways

- **Responsibility looks inward; Accountability looks outward:** Always face the client when there is a failure.
- **Never Transfer Blame:** While assigning internal responsibility is necessary for process correction, it must never be done in the client's presence or as an excuse to senior management.
- **Accountability is Promotion Material:** Leaders are defined by their willingness to own the outcome. Bankers who consistently make things right, even when the mistake wasn't directly theirs, are marked for advancement.
- **The Two Questions:** When a failure occurs, the responsible person asks, "Who did this?" The accountable person asks, "How do we prevent this for the client immediately, and how do we fix the system?"

Quick Action Plan: The 'Accountability Shield'

1. **Stop the Blame:** When a problem surfaces, immediately stop searching for "who" and pivot to "what" (the systematic error) and "how" (the client solution).
2. **Contact the Client:** Reach out to the client, apologize for the bank's failure, and personally guarantee the mitigation—even if the error was in a different department.
3. **Implement the Fix:** Focus internal communication not on disciplinary action, but on creating a systemic safeguard (e.g., a mandatory dual-check on all LCs).

Mental Tattoo

Responsibility runs the task,
Accountability owns the result.

CHAPTER 33

Trust vs. Authority - The Strategic Difference Between Influence from Position and Influence from Character

---

THE ANCHOR

"Authority can compel action, trust earns commitment". — Author

---

In every client interaction, the banker attempts to wield influence. Authority is influence derived solely from one's formal position, title, or the sheer size and reputation of the bank's brand (e.g., "The Global Head of M&A says we must do this"). Authority is hierarchical, external, and coercive—it compels action through perceived power. Trust, conversely, is influence derived from proven competence, integrity, and a history of shared experience (e.g., "I will follow this advice because this individual has consistently prioritized my interest"). Trust is earned, internal, and persuasive—it enables action through conviction. The strategic banker understands that Authority opens the door; Trust closes the deal and secures the loyalty.

The Use Case Example: The Generational Asset Sale in Mumbai

Meet Mr. and Mrs. Kulkarni, owners of a highly successful, generational manufacturing business in Mumbai, who are seeking advisory services to sell their company. They are not focused only on price; they care deeply about their family's legacy. Two banks pitch for the mandate:

- **The Authority Trap:** Mr. Sharma, a Senior Director from a globally renowned American investment bank, leads the pitch. He relies heavily on his Authority, using a glossy presentation filled with global tombstone deals and his own senior title, operating on the assumption that his brand itself is a sufficient justification. He dictates a fixed, top-down valuation model and pushes the bank's standard, high-fee structure as "market practice," leaving little room for dialogue. Legacy concerns, employee continuity, and post-sale control are acknowledged but not meaningfully explored. The Kulkarni's are impressed by the power of the brand, yet feel pressured, spoken to rather than listened to, and ultimately unheard.
- **The Trust Solution:** The competitor, Ms. Riya, was a less-senior Relationship Manager from a smaller, local investment firm. She did not win the meeting on brand power; she earned it through deliberate, patient trust-building over six months. Before any pitch was discussed, Riya invested time understanding the family dynamics behind the balance sheet. She met the Kulkarni's multiple times without presenting a mandate—listening to their concerns around succession, post-sale employee security, and the emotional difficulty of letting go of a business built over generations. She connected them, at no fee, to a succession-planning lawyer and a family governance advisor to help structure roles for the next generation, even if the sale did not proceed.

  Riya also commissioned a bespoke buyer-mapping exercise at her firm's cost, identifying not just the highest bidders but the *right* strategic buyers—those with a history of retaining Indian management teams and protecting legacy brands. She shared this analysis upfront, without locking the family into an engagement. When she finally pitched, she did not dictate valuation or fees. Instead, she framed trade-offs transparently: which buyers would maximize price, which would preserve culture, and which would offer long-term security for employees. Her influence came not from certainty, but from credibility built through prior action. The Kulkarni's ultimately chose Ms. Riya—not because she had the biggest brand or the highest title, but because she had already behaved like a steward of their legacy before being paid. Her Trust capital outweighed the Authority of a marquee institution.

The failure point is believing that a title can replace conviction. The strategic success lies in understanding that trust is the only currency clients will use to transact on their most valuable assets.

The Strategic Distinction

Authority is granted by the bank; Trust is earned from the client.

Aspect	Authority (The Coercive Power)	Trust (The Persuasive Capital)
Source	**Position:** Title, Brand, Hierarchy, or Regulatory Power.	**Character:** Proven competence, integrity, and shared experience.
Mechanism	**Coercion:** Compelling action through pressure or institutional weight.	**Persuasion:** Enabling action through client conviction and belief.
Resilience	**Fragile:** Lost the moment the title changes or the brand falters.	**Enduring:** Remains even when the banker moves to a new institution.

Aspect	Authority (The Coercive Power)	Trust (The Persuasive Capital)
High-Value Impact	Can open the **initial meeting** with the client.	Can secure the **final signature** on the advisory contract.

The Strategic Analogy: The Signature and the Seal

Authority is the official seal on the document—it grants permission and formal legitimacy. Trust is the signature the client chooses to put on the page. No matter how powerful the seal, a deal is never completed without the client's signature. Authority may open the process; Trust closes the commitment.

Key Takeaways & The Banker's Toolkit

Key Takeaways

- **Trust Trumps Title.** In high-value, complex deals, clients buy people and their integrity, not just prestige.
- **The Trust Audit:** If your client only follows your advice because they fear defying your bank's brand, you have Authority, but no Trust.
- **Trust is Portable.** A network built on Trust moves with you to your next role; influence built on Authority vanishes the moment you resign.
- **Wield Authority Sparingly.** Use your position to empower your team and expedite service, not to pressure or intimidate the client.

Quick Action Plan: The 'Trust Builder'

1. **Lead with Vulnerability:** When pitching, start by acknowledging a mistake you or the bank made in the

past and how it was fixed. This builds trust by showing honesty.

2. **Offer Pro Bono Value:** Once per quarter, give the client advice or a service that has zero fee attached (e.g., a strategic introduction, a non-bank market insight). This proves your interest is not purely transactional.
3. **The Title Test:** Whenever you advise a client, mentally strip your title away. Would the client still follow the advice based purely on the merit and your presentation of the facts?

Mental Tattoo

Authority is power,
Trust is influence.

CHAPTER 34

Delegation vs. Dumping - The Strategic Way to Empower or The Easy Way to Offload

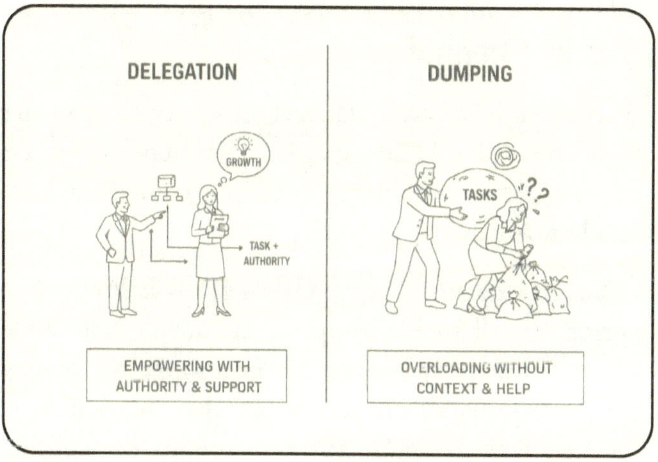

THE ANCHOR

"Delegation multiplies capability. Dumping merely relocates effort."— Author

---

In leadership, Delegation is the foundational skill for scale; Dumping is the fastest path to team fatigue and operational failure. In banking—where outcomes depend on multiple teams across credit, operations, compliance, and relationship management—no leader succeeds alone. Delegation is the strategic assignment of a task to a subordinate, accompanied by the necessary authority, resources, and clear success criteria. It is a tool for developing your team and freeing senior bandwidth for judgment-heavy decisions. Dumping, by contrast, is the careless transfer of workload without context, authority, or support—often disguised as "efficiency." It transfers work without ownership—leaving the task behind, but abandoning the outcome. The strategic banker understands that Delegation builds capacity and trust; Dumping creates resentment and guarantees a poor outcome.

The Use Case Example: The Complex Client Analysis in Chennai

Meet Karthik, a Mid-level Manager in Chennai, who needs a complex Competitive Landscape Analysis prepared for a high-value client meeting next week. He has a competent but busy junior analyst, Anjali.

- **The Dumping Trap (Offloading Effort):** Karthik prints the client file, drops it on Anjali's desk, and says, *"Get this done by Friday. It's the analysis the client asked for."* He provides no context on the client's actual pain points, fails to secure Anjali access to the confidential internal databases needed for the data pull, and assumes she will figure it out. Karthik has prioritized offloading his effort (Dumping) and has effectively *abdicated* the responsibility for the outcome. Anjali is overwhelmed, lacks resources, and the quality of the final report is predictably poor, requiring Karthik to redo it himself.
- **The Delegation Solution (Empowering Success):** Karthik assigns the task and says, *"Anjali, this is crucial. The goal isn't just data (the task); the goal is the one key insight that makes the client trust us (the outcome)."* He then proactively:

  1. Grants her temporary access credentials to the high-level research terminals.

2. Sets a clear mid-week check-in to review the initial findings.
3. Tells her to CC him on all communication with the internal research team, giving her authority.

Karthik Delegated the task, retaining ultimate Accountability. Anjali felt empowered, secured the necessary resources, and delivered a high-quality report, growing her own competence in the process.

The failure point is believing that getting a task off your plate equals success. Success lies in ensuring the *task is completed effectively* by the right person.

The Strategic Distinction

Delegation is assignment with support; Dumping is offloading without ownership.

Aspect	Dumping (The Offload Strategy)	Delegation (The Empowerment Strategy)
Motive	Driven by **Self-Interest:** Getting rid of work or avoiding responsibility.	Driven by **Growth/ Efficiency:** Developing the team and optimizing the leader's time.
Resources	**Zero:** Provides the task but withholds the necessary authority, time, or information.	**Provided:** Grants the necessary **Authority** and **Context** to ensure success.
Accountability	**Shifted:** The dumper blames the delegate when the task fails.	**Retained:** The delegator owns the final outcome (Accountability) but entrusts the task (Responsibility).

Aspect	Dumping (The Offload Strategy)	Delegation (The Empowerment Strategy)
Team Impact	**Creates Resentment** and low morale; stifles junior development.	**Builds Trust** and develops future leaders; frees up senior time.

The Strategic Analogy: The Financial Relay Race

Dumping is handing the baton to a teammate and walking away from the track, assuming they will win the race. Delegation is handing the baton to a teammate while remaining on the track to coach them, clear obstacles for them, and cheer them across the finish line. The focus is on the team's shared success.

Key Takeaways & The Banker's Toolkit

Key Takeaways

- **Delegation is an Investment.** The time spent setting clear success criteria is recouped ten-fold by the quality of the output and the growth of your team.
- **The Authority Principle:** Never delegate a task without delegating the corresponding level of authority needed to execute it.
- **Dumping is False Economy.** The short-term time saved by dumping a task is always lost in the long-term cost of re-work, error correction, and low morale.
- **Never Delegate a Crisis.** Tasks that require immediate, high-stakes political or ethical navigation must be handled by the accountable leader.

Quick Action Plan: The '3 Cs of Delegation'

1. **Context:** Explain the *Why*—the strategic purpose of the task and the client's ultimate objective.
2. **Clarity:** Define the *What*—the exact, measurable criteria for success (e.g., "The output must be a two-page summary with three specific action items").
3. **Check-in:** Schedule the *When*—a defined, mandatory mid-point review to course-correct, preventing the junior from failing privately.

Mental Tattoo

Delegation retains accountability,
Dumping abandons the outcome.

CHAPTER 35

Mentor vs. Sponsor - The Strategic Difference Between Advice and Advocacy

---

THE ANCHOR

"A mentor helps you see what you can become. A sponsor decides when the world gets to see it." — Anonymous

---

In every elite career, growth happens in two distinct phases. The first phase is competence—learning how to think, decide, communicate, and perform at a high standard. This phase is built through Mentorship. The second phase is progression—being trusted with visibility, risk, and promotion. This phase is unlocked through Sponsorship.

A Mentor is a seasoned professional who provides counsel, guidance, and perspective based on past experience. Mentors help you sharpen judgment, avoid mistakes, and strengthen your internal architecture. They improve *how* you operate. A Sponsor, by contrast, is a senior leader who uses personal authority and political capital to actively advocate for you—assigning you high-stakes projects, defending you in closed-door meetings, and backing your advancement when decisions are made without you in the room. Sponsors improve *where* you go. The strategic banker understands the critical distinction: Mentor talks to you about your potential and Sponsor talks to others about your promotion. Mentorship prepares you. Sponsorship moves you.

The Use Case Example: The Missing Promotion in Hyderabad

Meet Rakesh, a highly competent Vice President based in Hyderabad. He consistently received excellent performance reviews, delivered results, and was widely respected by peers. Yet, year after year, he was overlooked for promotion to Director.

- **The Mentor Trap (Advice, No Advancement):** Rakesh had an exceptional Mentor—Ms. Shreya. She coached him on presentation polish, stakeholder management, internal politics, and long-term career thinking. Her guidance strengthened Rakesh's decision-making and confidence. However, Ms. Shreya sat two levels below the Managing Directors who made final promotion decisions. She never spoke Rakesh's name in those rooms. Rakesh had all the advice he needed—but no one advocating for him when it mattered most. Rakesh didn't stall because he lacked guidance. He stalled because mentorship has a ceiling in hierarchical organizations.

- **The Sponsor Solution (Advocacy and Opportunity):** Recognizing this, Rakesh deliberately shifted strategy. He identified Mr. Vikram, a senior Executive Director known for backing talent and owning high-stakes mandates. Rakesh didn't ask Mr. Vikram for advice. He asked for opportunity.

  Specifically, he volunteered to lead the bridge financing for the Jupiter Energy deal—a complex, visible, and reputationally risky assignment. Rakesh executed flawlessly under pressure. The success gave Mr. Vikram both evidence and conviction. In the closed-door promotion discussion, Mr. Vikram stated plainly: *"Rakesh isn't just ready. He led the Jupiter mandate end-to-end. I trust him, and I'm backing him."* That moment—Mr. Vikram staking personal credibility—was Sponsorship. The promotion followed.

The failure point is believing competence alone drives advancement. Competence earns advice (Mentorship); taking calculated career risks earns advocacy (Sponsorship).

The Strategic Distinction

A Mentor improves your internal skill set; a Sponsor improves your external opportunity set.

Aspect	Mentor (The Guide)	Sponsor (The Advocate)
Focus	**Advice:** Internal development, skills, perspective, and navigating politics.	**Action:** External visibility, promotion, high-stakes assignments, and protection.
Relationship	**One-Way:** Driven by the mentee seeking help and guidance.	**Mutual:** Driven by the Sponsor investing in the protégé's success for the firm's benefit.
Risk Taken	**Zero:** Provides non-committal advice.	**High:** Uses personal political capital and reputation to back the protégé.
Goal	To make you **Competent** and **Knowledgeable**.	To make you **Visible** and **Promoted**.

The Strategic Analogy: The Financial Product Launch

Mentorship is running the model—stress-testing assumptions, refining logic, and ensuring the recommendation is internally robust. Sponsorship is standing in front of the Investment Committee, attaching your name and credibility to that model, and saying: *"I back this. Fund it."*

- If the model fails, the mentor's guidance is questioned.
- If the model fails, the sponsor's judgment is questioned.
- Both matter and build capacity. Only one creates momentum.

Key Takeaways & The Banker's Toolkit

Key Takeaways

- **Mentors are sought; Sponsors are earned:** You earn a Sponsor by proving your competence and capacity for high-risk, high-reward assignments.
- **Never Ask a Sponsor for Advice.** Ask them for an Opportunity. Advice is the Mentor's job; the Sponsor's job is to create the path.
- **Sponsorship is a Two-Way Street.** The Sponsor takes a career risk; your success must repay that risk by making the Sponsor look strategically sound.
- **Build Your Bench.** You need multiple Mentors for various areas (technical, political, life skills) and at least one high-level Sponsor for career acceleration.

Quick Action Plan: The 'Sponsorship Strategy'

1. **Identify the Target:** List the top five leaders who are in the rooms where your promotions are decided.
2. **Analyze the Need:** Identify a current, high-visibility business problem that the target Sponsor is directly responsible for solving.

3. **Propose the Solution:** Approach the target with a clear, concise proposal to lead the *execution* of the solution to their problem. This is how you ask for a high-stakes assignment—the currency of Sponsorship.

Mental Tattoo

Mentorship makes you capable,
Sponsorship makes you consequential.

CHAPTER 36

Revenue vs. Margin - The Difference Between Activity and Sustainable Profitability

---

THE ANCHOR

Revenue is vanity, profit is sanity, cash is reality." — Anonymous

---

In banking, growth is often celebrated loudly, but profitability is understood quietly. Revenue is visible, easy to measure, and politically attractive. Margin is subtle, harder to defend, and far more decisive. Many bankers build impressive books of business yet struggle to explain why their portfolios consume disproportionate capital, attention, and risk.

The strategic leader understands this truth: Revenue reflects activity; Margin reflects judgment. Revenue keeps the engine running. Margin determines whether the journey is worth taking. This chapter draws the line between bankers who stay busy and bankers who build enduring, profitable franchises.

The Use Case Example: The Volume Hunter vs. The Value Alchemist

Two Branch Heads in a major Indian Commercial Bank, Ravi and Smita, were evaluated during the quarterly review.

- **The Role trap (The Stalled specialist):** Ravi executed a high-volume strategy, acquiring numerous clients with large, simple working capital loans and basic transactional accounts. While his high top-line Revenue was necessary for market presence and competitive scale, his clients were rate-sensitive, operationally heavy, and required frequent firefighting. Revenue was high, but pricing power was low. Ravi prioritized maximizing the number of clients and transactions.

- **The Identity solution (The evolving leader)** : Smita pursued a margin-led strategy. She onboarded fewer clients but structured each relationship deliberately—bundling advisory, trade finance, risk solutions, and selective cross-selling. Her book generated lower gross revenue than Ravi's, but far higher risk-adjusted profitability. Her clients stayed longer, negotiated less, and consumed fewer internal resources. Smita understood that while initial volume is required in a competitive space, the long-term strategic focus must be on the quality of return.

When senior management reviewed return on capital, operational load, and client stickiness, Smita's portfolio emerged as structurally stronger. Ravi had built scale. Smita had built a business. The distinction became clear: Revenue showed effort; Margin revealed strategy.

The failure point is mistaking activity for progress. Leaders who optimize for revenue alone gradually train the organization to chase volume without understanding economics. Over time, pricing discipline erodes, weak clients dominate attention, and complexity multiplies faster than profit. The institution becomes busy, visible, and strategically hollow—working harder every year to earn the same return. Revenue grows; strategic control quietly disappears.

The Strategic Distinction

This is the fundamental operational pivot. Revenue (the top line) is a measure of activity; Margin (the bottom line) is a measure of strategic discipline, value creation, and pricing power. Both are valid and interconnected: Volume is necessary for market presence, but quality of return dictates the portfolio's destiny. The choice reflects an individual banker's central strategic alignment.

Aspect	Revenue (The Top Line)	Margin (The Bottom Line)
Metric	Gross volume of transactions or sales (how much money came in).	Net profit after costs, risk, and capital are factored (how much money was truly kept).
Focus	Volume, market visibility, short-term sales cycles, high activity.	Value pricing, cost efficiency, deep risk management, and client lifetime value.
Strategic Choice	To create **market presence** and competitive scale through volume.	To create **sustainable profitability** and long-term business viability through value.
Reward	Wins internal volume awards and short-term recognition.	Wins the long-term financial payoff and drives shareholder value.

The Strategic Analogy: The Financial Fitness Analogy

Revenue is weight lifted in the gym—it shows effort and intensity. Margin is functional strength—it determines whether the body performs under stress. Lifting heavier weights looks impressive. Moving efficiently, sustainably, and injury-free is what keeps you in the game. Senior leaders don't reward effort alone. They reward endurance.

Key Takeaways & The Banker's Toolkit

Key Takeaways

- **Margin is the Metric of Mastery:** It proves that you charge for value and that you understand the true, sustainable economics of your business.
- **Volume as a Foundation:** Initial volume is often necessary to establish a foothold in a competitive market, but it must be managed as a precursor to margin, not an end goal.
- **Pricing Power:** High-margin relationships grant you the independence and authority to advise without constantly defending your fees, aligning with your strategic focus.

Quick Action Plan: The Bottom-Line Pivot

1. **Margin Filter:** Before pursuing any deal, calculate the estimated *net margin* and risk-adjusted return, not just the gross revenue potential.
2. **Value Audit:** Identify the top 5 clients you serve who contribute the highest net margin, and allocate 50% of your time specifically to servicing and expanding those relationships.
3. **Pricing Discipline:** Know your minimum acceptable margin and possess the courage to walk away from business that falls below it, no matter the revenue size.
4. **Cost Review:** Track and calculate the true operational cost (time, resource use, risk capital) associated with your highest-revenue, lowest-margin clients.

The Bottom-Line Pivot

Review the last six months of closed deals.

Identify the lowest-margin 20% of your portfolio.

Decide deliberately:

- Reprice
- Restructure
- Or exit

Reclaim that time and capital for high-quality relationships.

Busy portfolios feel productive. Profitable portfolios build careers.

Mental Tattoo

Revenue can be grown,
Margin must be defended.

CHAPTER 37

Market Share vs. Mind Share - The Difference Between Transactional Volume and Trusted Authority

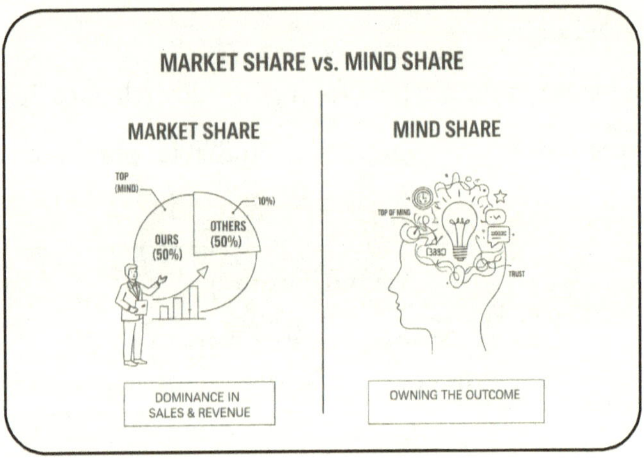

THE ANCHOR

"People don't choose the best product. They choose the product they understand the most." — Rory Sutherland

---

In banking, scale is visible; trust is invisible—but decisive. Market Share tells you how many clients transact with you. Mind Share tells you who clients instinctively turn to when the decision carries risk, consequence, and permanence. Market Share can be purchased—with aggressive pricing, balance-sheet muscle, distribution reach, or temporary concessions. Mind Share cannot. It must be earned slowly, reinforced consistently, and often without any immediate commercial payoff. Many institutions dominate league tables yet remain interchangeable. A select few command only a fraction of the volume—but shape outcomes far beyond their size. The strategic banker understands the order clearly. Market Share opens doors; Mind Share decides who gets invited back.

The Use Case Example: The Advisory Battle for the Tech IPO

A fast-growing Indian software company preparing for a landmark IPO shortlisted two banks for its lead advisory role. The competition narrowed down to two banks: Bank A and Bank B.

Bank A, represented by Vikram, was the category leader in Market Share. He dominated tech-sector lending, offered highly competitive pricing, and ran a well-oiled transactional machine. His pitch focused on execution strength, balance sheet size, and the ability to underwrite large volumes quickly. The strategy was clear: win the transaction, protect the volume, defend the relationship later.

Bank B, represented by Priya, had a smaller balance sheet and limited lending exposure. But over four years, Priya had quietly built Mind Share. She regularly shared forward-looking insights on SEBI regulatory shifts, talent retention risks post-IPO, and potential strategic buyers—without asking for mandates. She helped the CFO think, not transact.

The Market Share Trap (The Transactional Dominant): When IPO structuring became complex—ESOP treatment, overseas investor alignment, promoter dilution—the CFO bypassed Vikram's deal team. Despite Bank A's ubiquity and presence in the ledger, they were viewed as an execution tool rather than a strategic partner.

The Mindshare Solution (The Trusted Authority): The CFO called Priya directly. Not to negotiate fees, but to validate judgment. Bank B ultimately secured the lead advisory mandate, while Bank A was relegated to a low-margin, execution-heavy loan role.

The lesson was unmistakable: Market Share wins the deal today. Mind Share wins the decision tomorrow.

The failure point is believing presence equals preference. Organizations that fixate on market share assume that frequent transactions create loyalty. They don't. They create familiarity without trust. When decisions become complex, risky, or reputational, clients bypass the most present institution and call the most trusted one. Market leaders often lose influence precisely because they confuse ubiquity with authority.

The Strategic Distinction

This distinction separates the transactional bank from the trusted advisor. Market Share is a quantitative measure of volume; Mind Share is a qualitative measure of trust and lasting influence. The 99% chase the volume; the 1% cultivate the perception.

Aspect	Market Share	Mind Share
Goal	To dominate the percentage of total transactions in a given market segment.	To dominate the client's internal frame of reference and first thought process.
Strategy	**Volume-based:** Competing primarily on price, scale, and broad accessibility.	**Value-based:** Competing on niche expertise, specialization, and emotional connection.

Aspect	Market Share	Mind Share
Measurement	Quantifiable data: Assets under Management (AUM), loan volume, client count.	Qualitative data: Client advocacy, word-of-mouth referrals, indispensable status.
Value Proposition	You are *a* solution among many, vulnerable to fee erosion and switching.	You are *the* trusted authority, insulated from price wars and deeply embedded.

The Strategic Analogy - The Financial Real Estate Analogy

Market Share is renting space on the client's balance sheet. Mind Share is owning space in the client's thinking. Rent can be renegotiated every year. Ownership compounds. Strategic bankers don't fight for shelf space. They earn mental real estate.

Key Takeaways & The Banker's Toolkit

Key Takeaways

- **Mind Share is Insulation:** The stronger your Mind Share, the less vulnerable you are to competitors undercutting your price. Trust beats price.
- **The Opportunity Cost of Volume:** Chasing Market Share often requires price wars and high operational costs, severely impacting margin (Chapter 30).
- **Indispensability:** Your goal is not to be an option, but an essential first call. This status is built on unique expertise, not product pushing.

Quick Action Plan: Cultivating the Mind Share

1. **The Indispensable Question:** In every interaction, ask yourself: *What value did I deliver that could not have been replicated by a robot or a cheaper competitor?*
2. **Advocacy Tracker:** Track not just new business, but how many unprompted referrals and personal introductions you received this quarter.
3. **Niche Expertise:** Stop being generic. Identify one specific, high-value niche (e.g., cross-border compliance for tech firms) and publicly dominate its intellectual space.
4. **The Follow-Up Audit:** Ensure 80% of your follow-ups are about providing *external, unsolicited insight* and only 20% are about your bank's products.

The 3 R's of Mind Share

1. **Relevance**

   Before every client interaction, ask one question: "What decision will this client soon face where my insight could reduce risk or regret?"

   Mind Share begins when you engage around future decisions, not current transactions.

2. **Reputation**

   Audit your last ten client conversations. If most were about pricing, documentation, or execution status, you are building Market Share, not Mind Share.

   Deliberately introduce at least one unsolicited insight—regulatory, strategic, or competitive—in every key relationship each quarter.

3. **Recall**

Measure success not by deals closed, but by calls initiated. If the client calls you before making a decision, you own Mind Share.

If they call only after deciding, you are still renting Market Share.

Mental Tattoo

Market Share is rented territory,
Mind Share is permanent capital.

CHAPTER 38

Talent vs. Team - The Difference Between Personal Achievement and Institutional Resilience

---

THE ANCHOR

"No matter how brilliant your mind or strategy, if you're playing a solo game, you'll always lose out to a team." – Anonymous

---

In the high-stakes corridors of banking, Talent is celebrated early and rewarded loudly. It is the visible spark—the "rainmaker" who closes the impossible deal or the analyst who builds the flawless model overnight. Individual brilliance wins quarters and earns promotions. But brilliance is also a single point of failure.

Teams are noticed late and valued quietly, yet they are the only force capable of building a franchise, protecting a client through a crisis, and surviving market disruption. While Talent creates Performance, the Team creates Continuity. The cold truth: Concentrated talent is concentrated risk. When outcomes depend on a few exceptional stars, the institution becomes fragile. True leadership isn't measured by the stars you attract, but by how the system performs the day a star walks out the door.

The Use Case Example: The Credit Portfolio Crisis in Mumbai and Delhi

Two Regional Heads in a large multinational Commercial Bank, Rajesh in Mumbai and Aisha in Delhi, managed similar-sized credit portfolios.

The Talent Trap (The Concentration Risk): Rajesh built his success around a handful of brilliant, high-profile Talents. These stars personally negotiated the largest deals and handled all critical client communication, centralizing all key knowledge in their individual client books. The shock came when one senior banker was headhunted. Credit renewals stalled. Client confidence dipped. Internal teams struggled to reconstruct deal rationale, covenants, and relationship history. What looked like strength was revealed as concentration risk.

The Team Solution (The Institutional Legacy): In contrast, Aisha focused relentlessly on building a resilient Team system. She cross-trained her relationship managers on diverse lending products, credit logic, client sensitivities and deal decisions were documented and shared and stored in a communal system not just private notes. When a similar star banker on Aisha's team resigned, the transition was seamless. The portfolio held. Clients stayed. The institution absorbed the change. The Team possessed the institutional knowledge, proving that success built on Talent is brittle, while success built on the Team is institutionalized, scalable Legacy. The purpose of leadership is not to attract stars who may leave, but to build a constellation that remains.

The failure point is concentrating success in people instead of embedding it in systems. Leaders who over-reward individual brilliance unintentionally build fragile organizations—where knowledge is hoarded, transitions are painful, and exits are destabilizing. The moment a key performer leaves, performance drops, confidence fractures, and clients feel the gap. What looked like excellence is exposed as dependency.

The Strategic Distinction

This distinction represents the final pivot in leadership. Talent provides individual excellence; Team provides collective resilience, scalability, and success that endures beyond any one person. The 99% manage individuals; the 1% build self-sustaining systems.

Aspect	Talent (The Individual)	Team (The Collective)
Focus	Individual performance, technical brilliance, personal recognition.	Interdependent success, knowledge transfer, shared outcomes, and process optimization.
Risk	High ceiling but vulnerable to single points of failure, burnout, and ego dependence.	Lower individual ceiling but possesses resilience, scalability, and institutional memory.
Leadership Role	**Manager:** Directly optimizing and directing the individual's specialized output.	**Leader:** Building and inspiring a culture that maximizes collective, synergistic impact.
Reward System	Based on personal metrics, individual sales goals, and hierarchical ascent.	Based on collaboration metrics, knowledge sharing, and collective problem-solving.

The Strategic Analogy: The Banking Control Tower

Talent is the ace pilot who can land a plane in a storm. A Team is the air traffic control system that ensures every plane lands safely—even when the pilot changes. Institutions do not scale by relying on exceptional pilots alone. They scale by building systems that make outcomes predictable, repeatable, and independent of any single individual. Strategic leaders build control towers, not heroes.

Key Takeaways & The Banker's Toolkit

Key Takeaways

- **The Exit Plan Test:** Relying too heavily on a single individual means you have outsourced your risk management. Great **Talent** is necessary, but sufficient success only comes from a great **Team.**

- **Institutional Memory:** When success is proprietary to one person's brain, it is not inheritable. **Team-based** systems ensure that valuable knowledge remains within the institution.
- **Culture over Capability:** The 1% prioritize collaboration and shared purpose over recruiting the absolute sharpest, but least collaborative, individual.

Quick Action Plan: Institutionalizing Success

1. **The 15% Test:** Ask yourself, "If my single best performer quit tomorrow, what percentage of our total performance would be lost?" The target should be below 15%.
2. **Knowledge Transfer Mandate:** Require every senior member to document and actively teach their core, specialized skill to at least two junior colleagues annually.
3. **Shared Metric Introduction:** Introduce one or two performance metrics that can only be achieved collectively (e.g., team-wide client satisfaction score or internal referral rate).

The 3 S's of Team Resilience

1. **Share**

   Ensure no critical client, process, or decision logic lives with only one person. If knowledge is private, risk is public.

2. **Systematize**

   Document not just *what* was done, but *why* decisions were made. Institutional memory matters more than individual memory.

3. **Stress-Test**

   Ask yourself: *"If my top performer exits tomorrow, does performance dip or continue?"*

   If it dips materially, you have Talent—not a Team.

Mental Tattoo

Talent wins deals,
Teams build franchises.

CHAPTER 39

Management vs. Leadership - The Strategic Difference Between Maintaining Systems and Inspiring People

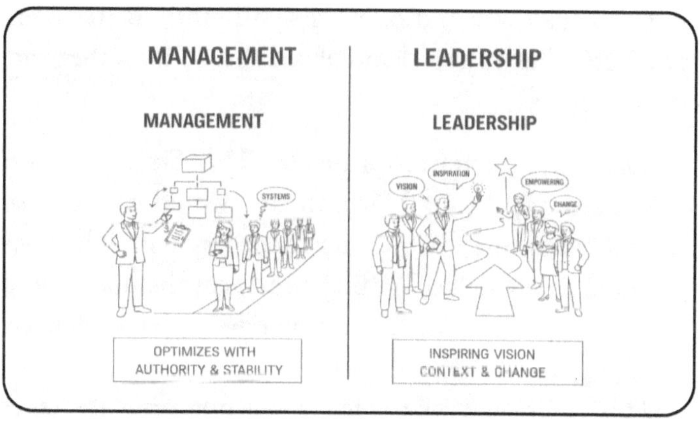

THE ANCHOR

"Management is doing things right; leadership is doing the right things." — Peter Drucker

---

In any organization, both Management and Leadership are critical, but they serve fundamentally different purposes. Management is the act of controlling, organizing, and optimizing systems, processes, and resources. It deals with *things*: budgets, spreadsheets, and procedures. It asks, *"How can we do this faster and cheaper?"* Leadership is the act of setting direction, inspiring vision, and motivating people toward a shared, compelling future. It deals with *people*: their potential, their beliefs, and their commitment. It asks, *"Why are we doing this at all?"* The strategic banker understands that you manage processes; you lead people.

The Use Case Example: The Declining Branch Profitability in Kolkata

Meet Meera, a Branch Manager in Kolkata, whose branch faces declining profitability due to a new, aggressive competitor opening a block away and offering significantly better rates on key products. The team is demoralized and believes they cannot compete on price.

- **The Management Approach (The Fix):** A manager, focused purely on Management, would tackle this by optimizing the existing, threatened system. They would immediately reduce staffing hours, cut the branch budget (cost-cutting reports), and implement a rigid new cross-selling quota (forcing existing clients to buy more). This is efficient Management—it optimizes the current, flawed system and addresses the budget crisis—but it destroys team morale and fails to solve the core problem of the competitive threat. The team is managed, but not inspired to win.
- **The Leadership Approach (The Purpose):** Meera, acting as a Leader, acknowledges the competitive pressure but pivots the team's mindset away from a losing price war. She gathers the team and asks, *"What is the one thing we can do that the competitor cannot copy?"*

  She then articulates a clear, practical vision: positioning the branch as the community's trusted financial advisor, not the cheapest lender. To make the vision tangible, she does three deliberate things. First, she redesigns weekly branch meetings—from pure target reviews to client-case discussions, where teams share one real client problem and how it was solved. Second, she reallocates time blocks, allowing relationship managers dedicated hours for proactive client reviews instead of constant walk-in firefighting. Third, she personally leads the first few SME workshops herself, signalling that this vision is not a slogan but a leadership commitment.

This is Leadership—it goes beyond motivating speeches. Meera converts purpose into visible behavior, rhythm, and role-modeling. By doing so, she restores confidence, gives the team a sense of control, and creates a differentiated strategy that competitors cannot replicate with pricing alone.

The failure point is applying managerial solutions (cost cuts) to a leadership problem (loss of purpose). The strategic success lies in understanding that people follow a compelling vision far more effectively than they follow a rigid checklist. .

The Strategic Distinction

Management optimizes the present; Leadership designs the future.

Aspect	Management (The Process Optimizer)	Leadership (The Visionary Mobilizer)
Focus	**Systems and Structure:** Budgets, processes, rules, and procedures.	**People and Vision:** Direction, commitment, motivation, and ethical culture.
Question	**How?** How do we execute this task efficiently?	**Why?** Why are we pursuing this goal? What is the purpose?

Aspect	Management (The Process Optimizer)	Leadership (The Visionary Mobilizer)
Role	**Maintains** stability and ensures compliance with current policy.	**Challenges** the status quo and drives change toward a new goal.
Impact	**Efficiency:** Improves the speed and cost of current operations.	**Effectiveness:** Drives the entire organization to a fundamentally new strategic destination.

The Strategic Analogy: The Financial Orchestra

Management is the act of tuning every instrument precisely, ensuring every musician is in the right chair, and following the notes on the page perfectly. Leadership is the composer and conductor: setting the emotional tone, inspiring the performance, and deciding the piece of music that the orchestra should play. The best performance requires both: perfect Management of the notes, and powerful Leadership of the vision.

Key Takeaways & The Banker's Toolkit

Key Takeaways

- **Be a Manager of Things, Be a Leader of People:** Your time must be split between optimizing the operational budget and inspiring your direct reports.
- **Management is Required; Leadership is Chosen:** You are hired to manage; you must choose every day to lead by setting direction and taking personal risk (Chapter 33).
- **Leadership is Communication.** When facing a crisis, leaders spend 80% of their time communicating the *vision* and 20% on the *process* fix.

- **Never Lead by Title Alone.** Leadership is not derived from your position (Authority, Chapter 35); it is derived from your ability to make others believe in the shared future.

Quick Action Plan: The 'L-vs-M Audit'

1. **Time Allocation:** Over the next week, track the percentage of time spent dealing with *processes* (budgets, emails, spreadsheets) versus *people* (mentoring, motivating, communicating vision).
2. **The Crisis Pivot:** When a problem arises, before jumping to the fix (Management), enforce a *5-minute pause* to define the vision and purpose (Leadership) of the solution.
3. **The Vision Test:** Before the next division meeting, remove all slides referencing last quarter's results (Management). Prepare only one slide defining the one major objective and why it matters to the team's legacy (Leadership).

Mental Tattoo

Management gets results through control,
Leadership gets results through commitment.

CHAPTER 40

Legacy vs. Success - The Strategic Difference Between Transactional Achievement and Enduring Impact

THE ANCHOR

"The greatest use of life is to spend it on something that will outlast it."— William James

Success is a finite, measurable achievement: the closed deal, the hit bonus target, the corner office. It is transactional, temporary, and personal. It is what happens to you. Legacy, however, is the enduring, perpetual impact you leave on your people, your institution's culture, and your clients' financial well-being. It is transformational, perpetual, and communal. It is what happens through you. The strategic banker understands that Success is what you take when you retire; Legacy is what you leave behind that continues to generate value. Legacy is the ultimate measure of Leadership (Chapter 38) and the culmination of all the principles—Integrity, Trust, and Simplicity—mastered throughout this book.

The Use Case Example: Two Retiring Executive Directors in Mumbai

The Investment Banking Division in Mumbai is preparing for the simultaneous retirement of two long-standing Executive Directors: Mr. Joshi and Ms. Sharma.

- **The Success Trap (The centralized Leader):** Mr. Joshi's career was a masterclass in individual performance. He was the primary architect of the bank's largest conglomerate relationships, but he operated on a model of exclusivity. By keeping client nuances and strategic "know-how" centralized within himself, he ensured he was always the indispensable pivot point. When Mr. Joshi retired, the "Institutional Memory" associated with his accounts went with him. Because the client trust was anchored to the man rather than the platform, the bank's grip on the portfolio became fragile. He achieved personal success, but the franchise he left behind faced a period of immediate uncertainty. His division's performance dropped 25% in the first quarter post-retirement. His career was a personal success, but he left an organizational void with no known legacy.

- **The Legacy Solution (The Institutional Leader):** Ms. Sharma delivered identical financial results, but she viewed her role as a Platform Builder. She practiced "Transparent Leadership," ensuring her Vice Presidents were not just executors, but co-owners of the client relationship. During her final years, she systematically transferred her credibility to her successors, positioning the bank's team as the primary source of value. Upon her departure, the transition was seamless. She didn't just leave a book of business; she left a high-functioning ecosystem of leaders she had mentored. Her legacy was a self-sustaining franchise that continued to grow, proving that her true value was the strength of the system she left behind. Her personal success was matched by a corporate Legacy of talent and enduring systems.

The failure point is confusing personal wealth with institutional value. The strategic success is ensuring that the process and the people you develop outlast your own tenure. .

The Strategic Distinction

Success is a score; Legacy is the character of the game you helped define.

Aspect	Success (The Transactional Win)	Legacy (The Transformational Impact)
Duration	**Temporary:** Lasts until the next quarter, year-end, or career move.	**Perpetual:** Endures for years through the people and systems you shaped.
Motive	**Ego-Driven:** Personal bonus, promotion, or status.	**Purpose-Driven:** Improving the client outcome, the team culture, or the industry standard.
Measure	**Quantitative:** Money, title, or ranking (KPIs).	**Qualitative:** The talent you built, the ethics you instilled, and the stability you created.
Focus	**Acquisition:** What you gained (clients, fees). **ROI:** Return on Investment	**Creation:** What you developed (leaders, systems). **ROE:** Return on Empowerment

The Strategic Analogy: The Financial Tool and The Toolmaker

Success is having the sharpest, most profitable financial tool in the market today (the high-performing deal). Legacy is being the master toolmaker: developing the people and the intellectual capital that ensures the bank can produce the sharpest tool for generations to come. The industry remembers the toolmaker long after the single deal is forgotten.

Key Takeaways & The Banker's Toolkit

Key Takeaways

- **Legacy is Your Ultimate Due Diligence.** The true quality of your career is measured by the performance of your team 12 months after you leave.

- **Invest in the Multiplier.** Dedicate 10% of your time to activities that have zero short-term fee benefit but create long-term leverage: mentorship, process documentation, and culture-building.
- **The System Outlasts the Superstar.** Build systems and empower juniors to run them; do not rely on personal brilliance that vanishes when you retire.
- **The Final Question:** On your last day, ask yourself: "Did I make this institution reliant on me (Success) or did I make it stronger without me (Legacy)?"

Quick Action Plan: The 'Legacy Builder'

1. **Identify the Successor:** Formally assign one high-potential junior to co-own your most valuable process or client relationship, delegating high-stakes tasks (Chapter 36).
2. **Codify the Principle:** Take the three ethical or operational principles you follow (e.g., "We always disclose the worst-case scenario") and write them down, ensuring they are adopted by your team (Chapter 32).
3. **The Exit Plan:** Create a formal 'Exit Document' that details not just your passwords, but the strategic philosophies you followed to succeed, leaving intellectual capital behind.

Mental Tattoo

Success is what you earn,
Legacy is what remains to endure.

Author Profile

Rishabh Chugh is a forward-thinking strategic leader who successfully bridges traditional financial rigor with the demands of the modern corporate and commercial landscape. With over ten years of experience, Rishabh has navigated complex roles across top multinational and leading Indian financial institutions. His strategic expertise spans key domains within commercial Banking for corporates, multinationals, software and technology companies, small and medium enterprises and the start-up & venture capital ecosystem.

His technical mastery encompasses transaction Banking and strategic growth through defining go-to-market strategies, implementing advanced initiatives, and exploring new revenue streams via strategic alliances. His career has been anchored in Bengaluru, the "Silicon Valley of India", providing him with an unparalleled vantage point for understanding the evolving financial architecture and strategic partnerships that drive the country's most innovative enterprises. Committed to staying ahead of the curve, Rishabh continuously monitors emerging trends, new technologies, and advanced strategies that ensure a dynamic, forward-thinking approach to banking.

This book, The 1% Banker Club, is an observation-driven guide based on a decade of distinction. Rishabh realized that the true differentiator among senior professionals was not their technical knowledge, but their daily, conscious micro-decisions. His work isolates the critical strategic distinctions that separate a merely competent banker from one who builds lasting value and legacy. He balances his professional life with the analytical pursuit of reading and writing, alongside the kinetic energy of sports.

Scan the QR code to connect and engage beyond these pages.

Stay in touch.

www.ingramcontent.com/pod-product-compliance
Lightning Source LLC
LaVergne TN
LVHW100307210926
848480LV00003B/1046